THE
GOOD
BOOK
COOKBOOK

NAOMI GOODMAN

ROBERT MARCUS

SUSAN WOOLHANDLER

Fleming H. Revell
A Division of Baker Book House Co
Grand Rapids, Michigan 49516

Published by Fleming H. Revell
a division of Baker Book House Company
P.O. Box 6287, Grand Rapids, MI 49516-6287

Library of Congress Cataloging-in-Publication Data

Goodman, Naomi.
The Good Book cookbook / Naomi Goodman, Robert Marcus, Susan Woolhandler.
p.   cm.
Includes bibliographical references.
ISBN 0–8007–1706–6
1. Cookery. 2. Food in the Bible.
I. Marcus, Robert, 1949–II. Woolhandler, Susan. III. Title.
TX652.G665 1990
641.5—dc20   89-71CIP360

Designed by Three's Company

Worldwide coedition organized and produced by Angus Hudson Ltd, Concorde House, Grenville Place, Mill Hill, London NW7 3SA, England
Tel: +44 181 959 3668
Fax: +44 181 959 3678

Printed in Singapore

Acknowledgments

We want to thank the many friends and colleagues who helped us to develop *The Good Book Cookbook* by sharing their expertise in different fields. First, Dr. George Landes, professor of Biblical Archaeology at Union Theological Seminary, our main consultant, who has been most generous with his time and knowledge. We would also like to express our gratitude to Rabbi Michael Robinson, the Reverend Richard Baggett Deats, Pearl Braude, Margaret Beach, Woodford Beach, Belle Goldblum, Percival Goodman, Rachel Goodwoman, Andre Lubart, Ruben Gums, Constance Prescod, Mary Marcus, Renee Marton, Victoria Marcus Martin, Paola Nivola-Silvas, Daniel Schley, Suzanne Sutin, John K. Sutin, Cynthia Vartan, Richard Wells, Barbara, Stephanie, and Anne Woolhandler, and finally, the folks down at Wolff Computer. Other scholars and cooking experts were consulted, but the final responsibility is that of the authors.

We also want to thank Alan Gilliam for kindly loaning authentic Middle Eastern properties; the expert home economist Catherine Lake; and the photographer Joe Morse of Unique Image Studio, London.

Special note

All recipes have been fully checked. for authenticity. They have also all been cooked and sampled.

Not all recipes are kosher. Some relate to pre-kosher times, others to New Testament times. For instance, the Roman banquet and Egyptian Banquet are certainly not kosher.

Contents

Foreword

Introduction

So he took butter and milk and the calf which he had prepared, and set it before them; and he stood by them under the tree as they ate.
Genesis 18:8

While the Bible does not give primary attention to the foods people ate or to how they prepared them for consumption, beginning with God's gift to humanity of plants and fruit for food in Genesis 1, to a reference to the twelve kinds of fruit on the tree of life in Revelation 22, there is hardly a biblical chapter that does not contain some allusion to various types of food, or to cooking and eating. Unlike some of their Babylonian predecessors or late Roman successors, the biblical writers did not record any recipes for the meals they often mention in passing. Yet through a careful study of the ancient Near Eastern literary legacy, together with an investigation of how more recent Middle Eastern culinary experts have prepared the same foods our biblical ancestors ate, it is possible to visualize what a number of these meals were like.

And that is what the authors of this book have brilliantly done. With painstaking research and an informed imagination, they have provided an authentic quality to the fascinating array of recipes they present. Moreover, when readers try out such delectations as Rebekah's Savory Stew, or Queen Esther's Pomegranate Walnut Sauce, or portions from King Solomon's Feast menu, not only will they discover some exciting new taste experiences, but they will also find themselves in closer touch with an important aspect of life as it was lived in biblical times.

As one who has enjoyed a sampling of some of the fare contained within the following pages, I can attest to the gustatory delight in store for those who likewise would fill their "hearts with food and gladness" (Acts 14:17). Indeed for me, as I would hope also for others, it has added a fresh dimension to understanding the invitation of the ancient psalmist: "O taste and see that the Lord is good . . ." (Psalm 34:8).

George M. Landes, D.D.
Professor of Biblical Archaeology
Union Theological Seminary

In *The Good Book Cookbook*, we invite you to enter biblical life through the kitchen door where you will discover a nourishing and often surprisingly sophisticated cuisine based on the Bible's many references to cooking and eating, generally amid settings of great rejoicing in the gift of food from God. Much of our information comes from these scriptural passages. We have developed recipes for specific dishes in the Bible, such as Esau's Pottage, Ezekiel's Bread, Roast Suckling Lamb, Fatted Calf, and Barley Cakes. Consulting biblical scholars and culinary experts, we have developed modern recipes for the meals eaten during this time, including royal feasts. We provide traditional foods for the religious festivals of the Hebrew Scriptures and the communal meals and holidays of the early Christians.

Our dishes are based on research into archaeological sources, biblical commentaries, classical writings, and the history of agriculture and food in the Middle East and Mediterranean areas. But as this book is a practical cookbook, recipes are listed under standard categories such as vegetables and desserts, not in historical sequence.

A healthful cuisine
The cuisine of the Bible is naturally a healthful one. It embodies the principles recommended by nutritionists and physicians today. All bread and grain dishes were of whole grain and all milling was done with stones; hence there was important fiber in the diet. Vegetarian and dairy meals were popular. Beans, grains, and raw vegetables were eaten frequently, as were yogurt and simple cheeses. Poultry and fish were far more commonly served than meat, which was generally reserved for special occasions. Fruits and nuts were the main ingredients in fine sauces and desserts. Refined sugar did not exist and is not part of the recipes in this cookbook, but you will find other unusual sweeteners made from dates, grapes, and, of course, honey

The site of the Holy Land— between the empires of the Fertile Crescent—made it a melting pot of culinary influences. And the extraordinary lives of many biblical men and women placed them in the royal courts of ancient civilizations throughout the Mediterranean and beyond. The time frame represented in this book begins around 3000 B.C. at the campsites of the early pastoralists, who roasted choice meats at

The busy fruit and vegetable market in Bethlehem.

their firepits and baked bread on heated stones. It concludes around A.D. 100 at the communal suppers of the early Christians throughout the Roman Empire. Along the way, you will sample the bakeries of Pharaoh's Egypt, the orchards of Babylonia, the spiceries of Persia, the health regimes of classical Greece, the elaborate banquets of imperial Rome, and the Last Supper of Jesus and His Disciples.

In the late Stone Age of Genesis, the families of Abraham, Isaac, and Jacob hunted wild birds, milked and managed their flocks, gathered the herbs that seasoned their foods, and tended their staple, still semiwild crops of barley, figs, and grapes. Savory stews, roasted lamb, grilled quail, fresh curd cheeses, macerated fruits, unleavened breads, and parched-grain salads are examples of the fresh "primitive" cuisine you will find in *The Good Book Cookbook*.

Advances in the kitchen arts came in Pharaoh's Egypt, along a fertile river valley famous for its abundant foodstuffs. The stonework of the Egyptian tombs has left us pictures of the kitchens, bakeries, gardens, and fisheries of the second millennium before Jesus. (Some carvings remain so detailed that poultry can still be identified from the markings on its wings.) Here in Egypt the arts of baking and brewing blossomed. Actual pieces of petrified bread discovered in recent times testify to the use of leavenings. The records of the Pharaoh Rameses III list over a million loaves of various breads presented to their deity, Amon-Ra, probably eaten by the slaves who built the pyramids. We tell you how to recreate the naturally leavened breads, some topped with onions, stuffed with figs, or flavored with exotic spices from the eastern caravans. A menu plan and recipes will enable you to prepare a sumptuous Egyptian-style banquet such as Moses would have known, distinguished by a variety of ducks, geese, and other marsh-loving fish and fowl. Our vegetable chapter suggests ancient ways to savor the succulent melons, pungent leeks, crisp radishes, and unusual lotus root dishes of ancient Egypt that caused the Hebrews to sigh with nostalgia in the Sinai desert after the Exodus (Numbers 11:5).

The rich soil of hillsides near Nazareth in modern Israel.

A distinctive cuisine

In the Promised Land, filled with milk and honey, wheat, grapes, barley, figs, and olives, the people of the Bible built a powerful nation-state founded on their unique religious principles. The principles, extending to the combining and handling of food, forbade the consumption of meat and dairy products in the same meal, thus distinguishing the cuisine of the Hebrews from all other Middle Eastern groups (although otherwise many of the same ingredients were used).

Our main objective is to gain insight into the daily lives of the people of the Bible through their unique methods of food preparation. We have tried to illustrate the differences in the cooking styles in the ancient Holy Land and the special relationship the Hebrews had with their animals, a relationship that governed the way meat and dairy dishes were prepared. We have, for instance, given examples of all the ways meat was prepared at the time, and you will find a number of unusual meat dishes, prepared with the wine, fruits, nuts, and herbs so abundant in the Holy Land. You will find a

An olive grove on the appropriately named Mount of Olives, Jerusalem.

wealth of fresh fruit and herb salads, vegetable casseroles, and hearty bean and grain stews. We present delightful calcium-rich dairy dishes and give simple directions for making your own yogurts and curd cheeses to serve with homemade biblical breads. You can choose from a variety of traditional seasoning agents and condiments of the Holy Land, such as black onion seed (black cumin), cumin, coriander, anise, cinnamon, cassia, must, grape honey, date syrup, rose water, orange flower water, capers, and ground pomegranate seed.

New foods
When the Israelites were conquered by Mesopotamia, Persia, Greece, and Rome, new foods and cooking styles were introduced. These empires have left written recipes and cooking records, which, generally concerned with the splendor of the royal tables, were often more explicit and detailed than those in the Bible.

The oldest known "cookbook" is a set of Mesopotamian clay tablets, originally thought to be a pharma-ceutical manual. As in all ancient cooking records so far discovered, there were no exact measurements given. And though the clay tablets of Mesopotamian cuneiform survived in greater numbers than the more fragile Egyptian papyri, the proper names of plants, spices, and condiments have been most difficult to decipher. Fortunately, a good translation exists of a list of produce from the gardens of the Babylonian King Merodach-Baladan, who is mentioned in Isaiah 39:1.

The Persians
The tolerant Persians were next to take over the Holy Land and its people. Consummate traders and seamen, with an empire that stretched almost to India, the Persians introduced new plants, animals, and spices to their subjects and perfected a cuisine of legendary delicacy and abundance. The Book of Esther begins with a Persian banquet that lasted for 180 days (Esther 1:1–6). Our selection of classical Persian foods will give you a taste of the culinary legacy of this empire.

As the people of the Holy Land became part of the Greek and Roman empires, their dining and cooking styles expanded. The classical records on botany, dietary customs, and food technology are quite extensive, and include the cookbooks of Apicius, *De Re Coquinaria*, believed to have been written around the time of the early Christian church.

The imperial Romans were fond of large and sumptuous meals, and were forced to pass laws restricting extravagant feasts. Inspectors even attended banquets to keep the menu selections within established boundaries. So, too, the temperate early Christians needed a reminder from Paul that dignified appetite was the standard for the communal meals of the church (Jude 12). You may also need a reminder of restraint when you sample some of the treats of these ancient repasts through the recipes and menu plans of *The Good Book Cookbook*.

Practicalities

All our recipes serve 6 unless otherwise noted. Some of the ingredients may seem unfamiliar and exotic, but most of our recipes can be made easily, thanks to modern technology. Never have we appreciated our everyday kitchen appliances so much as when we mulled over the long hours the biblical homemakers spent parching, grinding, salting, drying, pickling, and otherwise preserving their harvest. Biblical cooks made everything from scratch, including the pots and pans.

Through this book we have tried to show you the seasonal rhythms of agriculture and the methods of food preservation that dominated ancient life in the Holy Land. To understand these methods is to understand the life-style of the Bible's people and eat a variety of satisfying meals at the same time.

We hope *The Good Book Cookbook* will bring to life some of the events recorded so eloquently in the Scriptures, many of which are noted in our recipes. Our biblical references to the harvesting, preserving, cooking, and consuming of food in everyday life are from the New King James Version. We hope that you will enjoy preparing and consuming biblical meals as much as we have enjoyed developing, testing, and eating them.

Kitchen Notes

1. PORTIONS. All recipes serve 6 unless otherwise noted, although baked products, breads and cakes, often serve a larger number.

2. SALT. These recipes are low in sodium. Unless salt is necessary for chemical reasons (as in baking), recipes say salt to taste.

3. OIL can generally be used in place of butter and is so specified in the text. However, butter has valuable texturizing effects in baking and is occasionally recommended for this reason. Olive oil has been found to have great health benefits. The best olive oil is the cold-pressed variety which has not been heated during processing, thus preserving valuable nutriments. For the same reasons, use only cold-pressed sesame oil, sold in some regular markets (supermarkets) and in natural food stores. Oriental sesame oil is far stronger and is not suitable for these recipes. Other neutral cold-pressed oils, such as safflower, may be substituted, but do not use peanut or soy oils, which have quite a different taste.

4. SPICES have more flavor if ground directly before using. Preground spices can be substituted, but, if your spices are not fresh, you may want to increase the amount.

5. PARSLEY always means the flat-leaved type, sometimes called Italian (or French) parsley, which has a stronger flavor than the curly kind. If using curly parsley, increase the amount slightly.

6. STOCK. The liquid in which foods are cooked contains nutrients and should be kept and used when making vegetable or meat stocks.

7. WINE SUBSTITUTES IN MARINADES. In marinating, fruit juice acts similarly to wine, breaking down tough connective tissues and enhancing flavor. Grape juice can be substituted for wine, in the same amounts.

8. WINE SUBSTITUTES IN COOKING. Recipes specifying wine can have fruit juice substituted in the same amounts. Grape juice is recommended especially. If very small amounts are needed, a mixture of half water and half vinegar can be used. Note that when wine is used in cooking, the alcohol evaporates, leaving only the grape taste.

9. VEGETARIANS will find a wide variety of recipes listed under appropriate categories. Note also that vegetable stock may be substituted for meat or chicken stock if desired.

Notes for English readers

In most instances fry when instructed to sauté.
Broil means to cook meat over gridiron.

IMPERIAL EQUIVALENTS

1kg	= approx. 2 pounds 3 ounces
500g =	approx. 1 pound 2 ounces
250g =	approx. 8 3/4 ounces
125g =	approx. 4 1/2 ounces
100g =	approx 3 1/2 ounces

1 English gallon = 1 1/4 American gallons
1 English quart = 2 1/2 American pints

1 litre = approx. 1 3/4 English pints
500ml = approx. 17 1/2 fluid ounces
250ml = approx. 9 fluid ounces

Nutrition and the Bible

Do you like honey? Don't eat too much of it, or it will make you sick!
Proverbs 25:16 TLB

Modern nutritional science recommends a diet similar to the one eaten in the time of the Bible: high in fiber and calcium, low in animal fat, with plenty of fresh fruits and vegetables. People often express pity for what they think were the near-starvation conditions of biblical times. This is not a true picture of the five thousand years that surround the writing of the Bible. There were famines, as the Bible records, but there were also many long periods of prosperity during which an abundance of healthy indigenous foods were enjoyed. Many archaeologists believe that a larger variety of cultivated and wild vegetable foods were eaten regularly than are typically available today.

Abundant harvests were considered a reflection of God's favor. In the Bible, fresh elemental foods are celebrated: the sweetness of fruit; the richness of milk, cheese, and olives; the heartiness of grains; the special qualities of almonds, grapes, figs, onions, cumin, and herbs. The Bible frequently draws metaphors from the blossom, fragrance, and cultivation of the plants that sustained everyday life.

Nutritionists and doctors tell us to return to this more natural way of eating. High fiber, low cholesterol, fresh food, and moderate meat intake—all the standards of modern nutritional wisdom are embodied in the ancient diet of biblical times. The refining processes that have robbed food of too much of its nutritional value had not been invented. The overrefinement of food is a recent development of the past 150 years.

A high-fiber diet

Every bit of grain biblical people put in their mouths was whole grain. Therefore, their diets featured abundant naturally occurring fiber. "White" sugar did not exist through all the centuries of the Old Testament, and when a small amount was imported into Rome from India during the time of Paul, it was sold by apothecaries as a digestive aid. Meat was eaten sparingly and rarely cooked with butter or cream sauces. The Book of Exodus forbids eating meat and dairy products in the same meal while Leviticus limits the consumption of animal fat, the first commandment of lowering cholesterol. The preparation of meat usually marked a religious or otherwise special occasion such as the parable of the prodigal son's return.

Protein needs were met by combining whole grains with beans, thus receiving the benefit of the complementary amino acids in each. In addition to whole proteins, this combination of whole grains and beans contains complex carbohydrates, vitamins, minerals, and fiber with no animal fat whatsoever. Adding the herbs, wild greens and other vegetables, seeds, nuts, garlic, onion, yogurt, and olive oil that biblical people used to flavor their food not only enhances the taste but also increases the nutritional value. Fresh vegetables were eaten every day as a matter of course. Doing without them caused great lamentation among the children of Israel as they wandered in the Sinai desert (Numbers 11:5).

A vegetarian diet

The chapters on whole grains and beans, vegetables and fruits, and on breads are particularly helpful in learning how to incorporate these foods into your daily living. Consider trying a biblical vegetarian diet for 10 days as did Daniel (Daniel 1) or more gradually incorporate vegetable proteins into your everyday meals. Let poultry, fish, eggs, or small amounts of dairy products add interest to the basics, as they did in biblical times. There is no better way of eating, no matter how abundant other food may be.

Why whole grains? Today's modern milling methods strip grain of its germ and bran. Considering that these are the basic sources of the fiber, vitamins, minerals, and essential oils, there is every reason why the bran and germ of wheat should be left in the flour. The lightness of white flour products represents the absence of these "heavy" nutritional assets. Even pasta, unless it is made of whole grain flour, has been unnecessarily depleted of its original nutrients.

Healthy eating

The biblical way of eating provides a standard of the healthy, moderate diet experts are telling us to reinstate in our daily living. In the Garden of Eden, God provides fruit and vegetables for Adam and Eve. And after the fall, vegetables are specifically directed as food (Genesis 3:18, ". . . you shall eat the herb of the field"). The Bible is full of praise for the bounty of plants given for food by God. On the other hand, great restrictions are placed on the use of animal foods.

The Bible celebrates the delicious, fairly irresistible taste of meat. In Genesis 8:20, 21 the aroma of roasting meat prepared by Noah is so compelling that God is moved to pardon man for his sins, agrees not to destroy the world, and permits the eating of meat with special restrictions. The Bible is very explicit about the circumstances that surround the taking of an animal's life. It was not a casual act predicated on appetite. The God-given life-flame that human beings and animals share must be revered at all times. The animal must be raised in healthy circumstances and allowed to rest on the Sabbath just as God rested. It must be spared unnecessary pain at the time of slaughter. Feelings for its own young must be respected.

The treatment of food animals was a collective and individual responsibility. In today's world, this is recognized by having our meat inspected by the government. We take for granted that meat is prepared in hygienic surroundings and checked for purity, an imperative that reaches back to the Bible. What about your individual responsibility to revere the God-given flame of life?

You may be motivated to reduce your animal-fat intake in order to unclog your arteries and reduce the personal risk of a heart attack. The damage that too much saturated animal fat can do to the circulatory system is already highly publicized. There are still more reasons to stop the casual overeating of red meat. Being more conscious of the life-flame of animals has been a part of the Judeo-Christian heritage for five

The narrow streets of Nazareth boast a well-used vegetable market.

thousand years. We all need to strive to lower the frequency with which we eat meat and appreciate its special qualities when we do partake.

Dairy produce

In biblical times, people regularly ate dairy products in the form of yogurt and yogurt cheese. Yogurt often topped vegetable dishes instead of the butter or sour cream used today. Seasoned yogurt cheeses moistened bread instead of mayonnaise or served as a highly flavored dip for fresh bread and vegetables. The lacto-acidophilus bacteria of yogurt are extremely beneficial bacteria. They retard spoilage in milk and the live cultures assist the immune system of the intestines and reproductive organs. The Dairy chapter has many easy, delicious recipes using yogurt.

Dairy products were consumed regularly in biblical times, but in small quantities. It is believed that the daily diet rarely contained more than 10 or 15 grams of animal protein, yet the regular use of lacto-acidophilus yogurt and yogurt cheese kept the beneficial bacteria replenished in the system. For yogurt to do its work, it must enter the body alive. Eating pasteurized or otherwise cooked sweetened yogurt does not give the full health benefits. The sugar of commercial yogurt also inhibits the calcium absorption from the milk. Buy only plain yogurt that contains active, living cultures as clearly stated on the container. Or make your own easily and less expensively from powdered nonfat milk, following our instructions in the Dairy chapter. Sweeten lightly with fresh or dried fruit or a little honey, or try one of the salad or yogurt cheese recipes.

Let these principles and recipes increase your motivation to eat more fiber, less saturated fat, more fruit and vegetables, and more calcium-rich low-fat dairy products. People ate well for thousands of years without overly processed foods, questionable chemical additives, and "miracle vitamins." Ironically, as we strip food of more and more nutrients, they are handed back to us as miracle cures like fiber and beta carotene. These nutrients, common to whole grains and yellow vegetables, existed abundantly in the human diet in their natural form for thousands of years. Imagine what biblical people would think of our new discoveries: that fresh vegetables and whole grains are good for us!

Eating fresh foods

It is becoming more and more apparent that nutrients need the presence of other natural elements occurring with them to work most effectively. Modern nutritional science is very young, and many more vitamins and essential elements may yet be charted. This is why eating a wide variety of fresh foods in as close to their natural state as possible is your best health insurance policy.

In biblical times the hard work was planting, harvesting, grinding, gathering, drawing water from the well, stoking the fire. Today this labor is greatly reduced by our modern technology. These recipes were selected especially for their ease of preparation. You will soon see that thanks to modern technology it is easy, quick, and convenient to prepare pure, healthy foods.

Perhaps you will have to do a little shopping in those natural food stores. Speak to your supermarket manager about ordering whole wheat flour, whole grains like barley, millet, and wheat kernels, and whatever else may be required. Many stores are setting up special departments for natural foods and organic produce. Store personnel are willing to order what you want to buy, especially if your request comes as the representative of a group such as your religious organization. Exercise your collective consumer strength to improve the availability of healthy foods in your neighborhood.

Let these foods remind you of the great spiritual epoch that gave us the Bible. To enjoy the fresh bounty of God's harvest is a privilege, not punishment.

Dairy

Curds from the cattle, and milk of the flock. . . .
Deuteronomy 32:14

So I have come down to deliver them out of the hand of the Egyptians, and to bring them up from the land to a good and large land, to a land flowing with milk and honey. . . .
Exodus 3:8

While meat was generally reserved for special occasions, dairy products sustained the people of the Bible daily. Milk, like honey, was considered a special food because it was produced by animals solely for the purpose of nourishment. The Bible specifically mentions the milk of cows and sheep (Deuteronomy 32:14), camels (Genesis 32:15), and goats (Proverbs 27:27). Milk was regarded as a physical and spiritual extension of the mother animal. Ancient Egyptian pictures show a cow weeping as her milk is taken while her thirsty calf looks on.

Pagan religions paid homage to the connection of birth, milk, and motherhood through fertility rites in which calves were cooked in their mother's milk. Ceremonies of this nature were forbidden the Hebrews by the injunction "You shall not boil a young goat in its mother's milk" (Exodus 23:19). This regulation is one of the cornerstones of the dietary laws, known as kosher or kasruth. It was interpreted as forbidding any use of meat and dairy products in the same dish or even at the same meal. This separation of meat and dairy meals differentiated the cuisine of the Hebrews from that of traditional Middle Eastern groups.

Yogurt and cheese

Fresh milk could not be kept well in the hot climate of the Holy Land. So the principles of fermentation used in wine making and sourdough baking were also applied to the preservation of milk. The result was yogurt and cheese. The Hebrew language of the Bible had three terms for dairy products, which roughly correspond to yogurt, soft cheese, and hard cheese. The original King James Bible translated all these terms as *butter*. The New King James Version uses the word *curds*, a closer approximation to the actual foods, which were similar to our yogurts and simple white cheeses. Butter was a common food, considered the staple of shepherds, but for cooking, olive oil was preferred.

A herdsman with his cattle at sundown.

Basic Fresh Curd Cheese (left) and Pressed Coriander Cheese.

Cheeses

Basic Fresh Curd Cheese

In biblical times every family knew how to make fresh cheese from the surplus milk of the sheep, goats, and cows they kept. As with many ancient technologies, this cheese making is neither elaborate nor difficult, but requires organization and patience. Cheese making concentrates the milk proteins, leaving a nutritious liquid, whey. One gallon of fresh milk makes 11/2 pounds of cheese and several cups of whey. Whey should be treated as a light stock: enriching to soups and stews, sipped plain or lightly flavored, and always refrigerated.

To make most cheese, use sour milk. Fresh unpasteurized milk is soured simply by leaving it out of the refrigerator uncovered, overnight. Standard homogenized, pasteurized milk is soured by the addition of *1 tablespoon vinegar or lemon juice to every 2 cups (600ml) lukewarm milk*.

Heat the sour milk over low heat until solids separate. The solid mass is called the clabber. Pour this into a strainer or colander lined with a double layer of cheesecloth. Place the colander or strainer over a bowl to catch the whey. Any clean, open-weave, undyed fabric may be substituted for cheesecloth (2 layers of wet paper toweling will do in a pinch). Let the cheese drip overnight or at least 6 hours. Form the cheese into small balls and eat plain or seasoned as in the following recipes.

Yield: 1 quart (1.1 litres) milk makes about 6 ounces (170g) of cheese.

Pressed Coriander Cheese

1 recipe Basic Fresh Curd Cheese, using 5 cups (1.4 litres) milk

2 tablespoons coriander leaves, minced (finely chopped)

This is a pressed fresh cheese. To the fresh curds add the minced coriander and knead into the cheese. Rewrap cheese in cheesecloth and flatten it with hands to make a patty about 4 inches (10cm) wide.

Place the wrapped cheese on a strong plate and weigh down with a heavy object, such as a cast-iron pan. Leave the weight on for at least 5 hours. The finished cheese will be a cake about 1/2 to 3/4 inch (10–20mm) thick. Remove from cheesecloth and serve as is or cut into bite-size pieces. Toasted pita bread and olives are good accompaniments.

Yogurt Cheese

4 cups (1 litre) yogurt

1/2 teaspoon salt, if desired

Salt the yogurt and pour into double cheesecloth, tie up the ends to make a bag, and drain about 24 hours. An alternative method is to line a colander or sieve with cheesecloth and let the yogurt drain into a bowl. The yogurt can be drained for up to 36 hours to make a firmer cheese. Roll cheese into little balls and serve as a finger food, or use as cream cheese. Serve with Sarah's Bread or Barley Cakes.

Yield: 2 cups (625g) of yogurt cheese

Fresh Cheese With Seed Relish

. . . parched seeds, honey and curds. . . .
2 Samuel 17:28, 29

3 tablespoons fresh squash (pumpkin) seed

1 tablespoon black or white mustard seed

1 teaspoon whole cumin seed

1 teaspoon poppy seed

1/2 pound (225g) fresh white cheese

Pinch of clove, cinnamon, and coriander

Salt to taste

2 tablespoons honey (optional)

In a heavy skillet (pan), roast the squash seed without oil until they begin to crisp. Stir frequently. Add the other seeds and spices; toast lightly until the mustard seeds begin to pop. Allow to cool. Sprinkle on top of cheese. Salt to taste. If a sweet version is desired, spoon honey on top of cheese and sprinkle with seed relish. Vary the proportions to taste. Serve with Whole Wheat Sourdough Bread, Lentil Pancakes, or Matzoh.

Cinnamon Cheese

Cinnamon was one of the earliest of traded commodities, caravanned across the desert by camels from the East. It was a favorite scent for perfumes and incense as well as a flavor for food (Exodus 30:23). Cassia, a cinnamonlike bark mentioned in the Bible, was also traded.

1/2 pound fresh curd cheese at room temperature (pot, farmer's cream, or yogurt cheese)

2 teaspoons freshly ground cinnamon (more if desired)

Pinch of salt

1 teaspoon honey or 2 tablespoons sweet grape juice

Combine all ingredients. Store in refrigerator. This cheese is excellent on toast. More honey may be added along with nuts and raisins if desired.

Basic Goat Cheese Yogurt Spread

1/4 cup (50g) tart goat cheese at room temperature

1 cup (300ml) yogurt

2 tablespoons olive oil

Black olives

Chopped pistachios

Parsley

Black cumin

Beat cheese and yogurt together into a smooth paste. Vary proportions to suit taste. Moisten with milk or cream if a liquid texture is preferred. Spread a thin layer of the sauce over a few small, flat plates. Drizzle olive oil over the cheese sauce. Garnish with black olives, nuts, parsley, or black cumin. Serve with Sourdough Fig Roll. A bowl of seasoned chick peas and a salad go nicely with this dish.

Ur: Green Butter Herb Cheese

For as the churning of milk produces butter. . . .
Proverbs 30:33

Butter was sometimes used to pay taxes in the Holy Land. Ur, an herbed mixture of cheese and butter, is an ancient combination that was especially popular with the Babylonians.

1 tablespoon each fresh chopped mint, parsley, dill, green scallion tops (spring onions), coriander leaves, arugula (rocket), thyme, and rue*

1/2 pound (225g) fresh curd cheese: cream, farmer's, or whipped cottage

1/4 pound (125g) butter

Salt to taste

Have cheese and butter at room temperature. Mash herbs, cheese, and butter together. Salt to taste. Let sit for an hour or store overnight in the refrigerator to let flavors mingle. Serve with Matzoh, Whole Wheat Sourdough toast, or over warm vegetables. Vary proportions to suit taste.

* Rue can cause dermatitis in people with sensitive skin, and can cause serious burns if the sap contacts the skin in warm weather. It can also cause abortion.

Hot Radish Cheese Spread

1/2 pound (225g) fresh curd cheese at room temperature

1 tablespoon grated fresh radish *and/or* 1/2 teaspoon freshly grated horseradish (more if desired)

Pinch of salt

Combine all ingredients. This is best served fresh. Fresh cucumber sandwiches made with radish cheese spread are excellent with cold drinks.

Opposite: Fresh Cheese with Seed Relish (left); Cinnamon Cheese (top) and Ur: Green Butter Herb Cheese.

Vine Leaves Stuffed With Cheese

30 vine leaves

3/4 cup (220ml) olive oil

3/4 cup (220ml) vinegar

FILLING

16 ounces (500g) of soft goat cheese, yogurt cheese, or a combination (see page 12 for directions on making yogurt cheese)

Cumin (optional)

SAUCE

1 cup (300ml) plain yogurt

1 tablespoon fresh basil, cut fine, or 1 teaspoon dried basil

1 tablespoon fresh mint, cut fine, or 1 teaspoon dried mint

1 clove garlic, mashed (optional)

Steam the vine leaves for 10 minutes if preserved leaves, 20 minutes if young fresh leaves. Combine olive oil and vinegar for marinade, heat to boiling and pour over vine leaves. Let marinate for at least 1 hour. Longer marination will make them taste even better. Pour off marinade and reserve for future use on more vine leaves, duck, chicken, or fish.

For the filling, the goat cheese can be used plain while the yogurt cheese may be sprinkled with cumin. The goat cheese will have a stronger flavor than the yogurt cheese.

Separate the vine leaves, lay several flat on a plate, and put a small amount (1 to 3 teaspoons full) of filling in the center. Make a package by folding the stem end over on top, then folding up the two sides, and last the pointed end. Continue until all the leaves are stuffed.

Combine the yogurt with the basil and mint, which are better fresh in this dish, and add the garlic, if using.

Serve the vine leaves with the sauce on top or on the side. As a first course, allow 4 stuffed vine leaves per person.

Stuffed vine leaves are an excellent addition to a buffet or tasting table.

Vine leaves prepared as in this recipe can be stuffed with cooked barley, cooked millet, or soaked bulgur, seasoned with cumin, mint, and basil, and served with the same sauce.

Fresh Cheese With Garlic and Herbs

4 cloves garlic, unpeeled (more if desired)

2 tablespoons olive oil

Parsley, thyme, and dill, fresh, totaling at least a tablespoon; if dried, 1 teaspoon

1/2 pound (225g) fresh curd cheese at room temperature

Salt to taste

Sauté garlic in 1 tablespoon olive oil, gently, until golden. Let cool. Peel and mash garlic with herbs and additional tablespoon of oil. Mix into cheese. Add salt if necessary. Let sit several hours before serving. Form cheese into balls or small cakes if desired. This garlic cheese and the Marinated Goat Cheese may be used in Hot Goat Cheese With Fresh Herb Salad.

Hot Goat Cheese With Fresh Herb Salad

SALAD GREENS

Include bitter herbs such as arugula (rocket), endive, watercress, and romaine (cos) lettuce.

1 cake per serving of Fresh Goat Cheese or Cheese With Garlic and Herbs, about 1/2 inch (65mm) thick and 21/2 inches (15mm) wide

1/2 cup (150ml) olive oil

1 tablespoon mustard

1 teaspoon honey

1/8 cup (30-40ml) wine vinegar

Fresh herbs: coriander leaves, thyme, dill

Marinate the rounds of goat cheese in about 1/4 cup (70ml) olive oil for at least 4 hours. Prepare a vinaigrette dressing with the mustard, honey, remaining olive oil, and vinegar. Put rounds of goat cheese on a baking sheet and bake in a preheated hot oven, about 425°F (220°C, Gas mark 7), for 5 to 8 minutes. Cheese should be bubbly and golden. Meanwhile, toss salad with vinaigrette dressing and put into individual bowls. As cheese comes out of the oven, slide 1 cake onto each salad bowl. Toss hot cheese into the greens. Serve immediately with bread or crackers.

Roman Broccoli Goat Cheese Soup

You shall have enough goats' milk for your food, for the food of your household. . . .
Proverbs 27:27

2 heads broccoli

5 cups (1.4 litres) water*

1/4 pound (125g) fresh goat cheese (more if desired)

Salt and pepper

Vinegar

Dash of cumin

Chopped scallions (spring onions)

Parsley or coriander

Chop broccoli and boil in the water for 10 minutes. Remove from heat. Add goat cheese to water and broccoli. Put through a blender, mindful that the texture of the vegetables in the soup can be varied from chunky to smooth. The goat cheese should be well creamed into the liquid. Taste. Add salt, pepper, and seasonings as desired. Serve immediately with croutons, bread and butter, and an unusual salad with colors other than green (for example, radishes, oranges, and olives).

Meat stock can be used in place of water, and cream may be added for extra richness.

Cooked Garlic, Cheese, Parsley, and Olive Salad Dressing

2 cloves garlic, unpeeled

1/4 cup (70ml) water

1/4 pound (125g) sheep cheese such as feta

1/2 cup (150ml) olive oil

1/4 cup (70ml) red wine vinegar

A handful of black olives, preferably oil-cured, pitted and chopped

Fresh chopped parsley

Boil the garlic cloves in the water for 2 minutes. Cool and peel. Put garlic, cheese, oil, and vinegar into blender. Puree. Add more water if you prefer a thinner dressing. Add olives and parsley. Taste before salting, as some cheeses such as feta are already quite salty. Serve on vegetables, salad greens, or as a dip.

Marinated Goat Cheese

Fresh cheese was covered with olive oil and spices to preserve as well as flavor it.

Up to 1 1/2 teaspoons total, more to taste: bay leaf (crumpled), celery seed, whole coriander, cumin seed, thyme, dill, fennel seed, black pepper

1/2 to 1 cup (250–400ml) olive oil

1 pound (450g) fresh goat cheese

Fresh parsley or coriander leaves

Select your favorite seasonings and stir them into the olive oil. Let steep for at least an hour. Form cheese into balls or cakes and arrange in 1 or more suitable containers for marinating. Pour flavored olive oil over cheese and let sit at least 1 hour before serving. If completely covered by oil, cheese may remain unrefrigerated for several hours. In the refrigerator, olive oil will congeal rather unattractively. Always bring cheese to room temperature before serving. Sprinkle with fresh parsley or coriander leaves. Serve with Matzoh, olives, and pickles.

Hot Goat Cheese With Fresh Herb Salad (left) and Vine Leaves Stuffed With Cheese.

Yogurt

Yogurt, like all thickened milk, was considered to be curds. Warm milk becomes infused with the healthy lacto-acidophilus bacteria and thickens. This ancient food has become very familiar in Western markets. Good yogurt can be purchased everywhere. However, a delicious, economical yogurt can be produced at home. Powdered milk makes a more consistent product than homogenized milk.

You will need yogurt starter. Yogurt starters can be purchased at health food stores, but we have not found them better than plain commercial yogurt.

Whole Milk Yogurt

1 quart (1.2 litres) milk

2 tablespoons plain yogurt or yogurt starter

Heat milk to the boiling point to kill unwanted bacteria, then cool to about 100°F to 110°F (37°C–43°C—slightly higher than the temperature of the human body; milk will feel warm to the wrist). Add yogurt starter. Mixture must be kept consistently warm to thicken. This can be done in various ways:

1. Put covered bowl in a pan of warm water over a pilot light on the stove or in an oven with a gas pilot light.
2. Put covered bowl on the floor next to a radiator or refrigerator exhaust.
3. Make yogurt mixture in a prewarmed wide-mouthed thermos bottle.
4. Use an electric yogurt maker, following directions.

About 8 hours is necessary for the milk to turn into yogurt.

Yield: 1 quart (1.2 litres) yogurt.

Powdered Milk Yogurt

Powdered milk makes more consistent yogurt than fresh milk.

Dissolve 2 cups (450g) powdered milk in 4 cups (1.2 litres) warm water. Add 2 tablespoons yogurt and follow directions for Whole Milk Yogurt.

Each succeeding batch of yogurt is made by using 2 tablespoons from the preceding batch. The texture and taste of yogurt will vary. Thin yogurt is excellent as a drink or can be used as stock in soup. After several batches of yogurt are made, the starter may need to be replaced.

Yield: 1 quart (1.2 litres) yogurt.

TO STABILIZE YOGURT FOR COOKING

Salted yogurt made of goat's milk may be used directly in cooking. Cow's-milk yogurt will curdle unless pretreated.

Up to 5 cups (1.4 litres) plain yogurt

1 egg white, beaten

3/4 teaspoon salt (use less salt for less yogurt)

Put all ingredients in a small saucepan and heat over a low flame, stirring in the same direction, until the mixture begins to boil. Turn down heat and simmer for 5 to 10 minutes or until thick. This yogurt can be used for long cooking without curdling (although an alternative is to stir in the yogurt after food is removed from heat).

Yogurt With Fresh Herbs and Cucumber

Mix fresh yogurt with "every green herb for food"
(Genesis 1:30).

2 medium-size cucumbers, thinly sliced (waxed cucumbers must be peeled or well scrubbed)

2 cups (600ml) fresh plain yogurt

Salt to taste

5 tablespoons or more chopped fresh coriander leaves, parsley, mint, dill, fennel, green onion tops, arugula (rocket), very young mustard greens

2 cups (600ml) buttermilk (optional, see below)

To serve as a soup: Combine all ingredients and let sit for an hour before serving. Chill if desired.

To serve as a sauce or relish: Omit buttermilk and, if desired, cucumber.

Yogurt Sesame Sauce

1 cup (300ml) plain yogurt

1/4 cup (70ml) sesame paste (tahini, see page 60) (more if desired)

1 to 2 tablespoons vinegar or lemon juice

Salt to taste

Sprinkle of herbs: fresh dill, coriander leaves, parsley

Combine all ingredients, tasting to adjust proportions. Use low-fat yogurt for an excellent low-cholesterol (though, unfortunately, not low-calorie) sauce for vegetables, sandwiches, and salads.

Opposite: Whole Milk Yogurt (top left), Yogurt Sesame Sauce (right), and Yogurt With Fresh Herbs and Cucumber (bottom left).

Yogurt Drinks

These drinks are as delicious on a hot day today as they were in biblical times. Dilute yogurt with cool water in a ratio of 1 to 2. Stir or whirl gently through blender with additional flavorings. Serve chilled.

MINT
This ancient combination is good salty or sweet. To a diluted yogurt mixture, add 6 sprigs fresh mint, chopped and crushed, and 1/2 teaspoon salt or 2 tablespoons honey.

COLD CREAMED BEET
Blend 1 small, cooked, shredded beet (beetroot) per cup of diluted yogurt (more if desired). Sweeten with honey if desired. The addition of rose water will make an unusual drink, brilliantly colored and redolent of flowers. Begin with 1/4 teaspoon of rose water and gradually increase to 1/2 teaspoon.

CITRON (ORANGE) FLOWER
The flavoring of orange flowers may have preceded the use of the fruit in the Holy Land. Sweeten diluted yogurt with 2 to 3 tablespoons honey and add 1/4 teaspoon orange flower water (more if desired). Garnish with mint.

POMEGRANATE
Add 3 tablespoons fresh or bottled pomegranate juice to diluted yogurt (more to taste). Sweeten with honey if needed. This drink also has a pale pink color.

DATE
Add 6 fresh or dried and soaked dates (pitted) to diluted yogurt. Blend and sweeten with additional date syrup if desired.

GRAPE
Sweeten diluted yogurt with fresh grapes or a combination of fresh grapes and Grape Honey.

CAROB
Mix a tablespoon of carob (-flour) with a small amount of water. Add 1/2 tablespoon honey (more to taste) and mix with diluted yogurt. Whirl through a blender.

Yogurt Cumin Seed Sauce

| 1 cup (300ml) plain yogurt |
| 1 teaspoon whole cumin seed |
| Salt to taste |

The flavor of this simple, piquant sauce is enhanced by roasting and grinding the cumin. Spread cumin seeds on the bottom of a cast-iron skillet (pan). Heat until toasted and fragrant. Crush in a small mill or mortar. Add to yogurt. Season with salt. This is an excellent sauce for vegetables and meats.

Yogurt Soup With Raisins

| 2 hard-boiled eggs, chopped |
| 3/4 cup (175g) raisins, soaked in 2 cups (600ml) cold water for 5 minutes |
| 4 cups (1.2 litres) yogurt |
| 1 tablespoon vinegar |
| 3/4 cup (220ml) milk |
| 2 cups (450g) diced cucumbers |
| 1/2 cup (125g) chopped scallions (spring onions) |
| 1 teaspoon salt |
| 1/2 cup (125g) blanched slivered almonds (optional) |
| 2 tablespoons parsley, minced (optional) |
| 2 tablespoons dill, minced (optional) |

In a large bowl, blend eggs, raisins, cold water, yogurt, vinegar, milk, cucumber, scallions, and salt. Refrigerate for at least 2 hours or heat and serve when thoroughly warmed. Do not boil. Garnish with herbs and nuts as desired. Serve with Matzoh, Onion, Olive, and Orange Salad, and Ashurey for dessert.

Chick Pea Yogurt Soup With Greens

Beets, mustard, and radishes were the popular greens of the Patriarchs. Spinach, introduced by the Persians, was known around the Mediterranean area by the time of Jesus. This recipe is simplified by using pre-spiced chick pea flour. Generally sold as falafel mix, it is moistened and made into fried patties called falafel. It is a popular meat substitute sold in health food stores and some supermarkets.

| 5 cups (1.4 litres) water |
| 3/4 cup (175g) falafel mix* |
| 1 cup yogurt (sour yogurt may be used) |
| 1 pound (450g) of fresh or frozen beet greens or spinach, cooked and drained |
| 2 tablespoons vinegar or lemon juice |
| 1 teaspoon black pepper |
| 2 tablespoons olive oil or untoasted sesame oil |
| 1 teaspoon whole cumin seed |

In a bowl, slowly beat 1/2 cup (150ml) water into the falafel mix or chick pea flour to maintain a smooth paste. In a separate bowl beat yogurt with remaining water to a frothy cream. Add the yogurt mixture to the chick peas slowly. Put in a heavy pot and simmer over medium heat. Add greens, pepper, and vinegar or lemon. Cover and simmer for at least 1 hour, stirring frequently. Add more water if necessary—the mixture will become quite thick. In a small saucepan, heat oil and add cumin seed. Sauté until aroma develops. Add to soup. Serve hot over Basic Barley or Millet or serve as a cold soup.

If falafel mix is not available, make your own. To powder your own chick peas, read instructions for Lentil Pancakes, page 30.

FALAFEL MIX
| 3/4 cup (175g) chick pea flour |
| 1 teaspoon ground cumin seed |
| 1 teaspoon ground coriander seed |
| 1/2 teaspoon turmeric |

1/4 teaspoon powdered ginger

1/2 teaspoon garlic powder

3 tablespoons parsley, dill, or mint, chopped

5 tablespoons sautéed or dehydrated onion (optional)

1/2 teaspoon ground pomegranate seed (optional)

Pinch of saffron

Black pepper

Persian Yogurt Soup With Meatballs

According to legend, Queen Esther was so strict in her following of the kosher laws that she ate only seeds and vegetables. However, when she gave a series of banquets to persuade King Ahasuerus to spare her people, she served Persian classics like this elegant soup.

SOUP

3 cups (900ml) yogurt

1/4 cup (50g) cooked millet or uncooked rice

1 egg, beaten

2 tablespoons whole wheat flour

1 teaspoon salt

1/2 teaspoon pepper

1 teaspoon dried dill or 2 tablespoons fresh

3 cups (900ml) water

1/4 cup (50g) parsley, chopped

1/2 cup (125g) cooked chick peas (canned may be used)

1/2 cup (125g) finely chopped green onions (spring onion tops)

MEATBALLS

1/2 pound (225g) ground beef, lamb, or veal

1 small onion, minced (finely chopped)

1/2 teaspoon salt

1/2 teaspoon pepper

HOT GARLIC SAUCE (OPTIONAL)

2 cloves garlic

1/2 cup (125g) melted butter

1 tablespoon dry mint or 2 tablespoons fresh

In a 2–quart saucepan, mix yogurt, millet or rice, egg, flour, and seasonings. Add water and stir. Simmer over a low flame, stirring occasionally, for a half hour. To make meatballs, mix meat, onion, salt, and pepper together in a bowl. Shape into small balls, rolling them between the palms of the hands. When the soup has thickened slightly, add parsley, chick peas, green onion, and meatballs. Simmer an additional 30 minutes, stirring occasionally. To prepare the garlic sauce, chop the garlic cloves and sauté briefly in melted butter. Add mint and stir well. At the table, put a spoonful of sauce in each serving of soup. Serve with Shaped Rolls and Haroseth.

Persian Yogurt Soup With Meatballs.

Whole Grains and Beans

*A land of wheat and barley, of vines and fig trees and pomegranates,
a land of olive oil and honey.*
Deuteronomy 8:8

Whole grains and beans were the sustaining daily food of the people of the Holy Land. The wild grasses that yield barley and wheat can still be found growing on the sunny hillsides as they did millennia ago. The beginning of grain cultivation involved a complicated merging of primitive technologies: Plows and hoes were needed to plant, pottery to store, and millstones to grind the grain. This process is considered the beginning of civilization, for as a result mankind developed a steady food supply and, in turn, stable communities. Flanking the Holy Land, Mesopotamia and Egypt possessed unique river systems that, by serving as means of irrigation, enabled the development of grain empires.

The irrigation methods of the ancient world have barely been surpassed today. Mesopotamia, now Iraq, was once the most fecund grain-producing area in the world. Its vast network of irrigation canals required careful management to prevent silting. Deterioration of the system came only after a series of wars that destroyed the central administration of the grain industry and general resolve of the populace. The fertility of the region has never been restored to the levels of ancient times.

Grain at every meal

Ancient people expected to see grain at every meal in one form or another: green, boiled and parched, soaked and roasted, malted into beers, and baked into puddings, flans, and casseroles. Grain was sprouted, pounded, dried, crushed, and reconstituted. But bread was a luxury, not a convenience food, in ancient times, because hours of laborious pounding, grinding, and sifting were necessary to make flour. Centuries passed before fine flours became common and inexpensive. In the meantime, the average family of biblical times ate a wide variety of porridges, pilafs, soups, and parched-grain salads.

God's grace

The people of the Bible saw the grace of God in an abundant grain harvest and feared His wrath would manifest itself in a famine. Hence, the close timing of grain harvests and religious festivals was not a coincidence; it was considered the spiritual rhythm of the universe. Rituals involving grain were part of the holidays. The barley harvest was in early spring, at the time of Passover; 7 weeks later the wheat was harvested at Shabuoth (Pentecost). Sheaves of wheat were laid upon the altar of God in thanksgiving. This identification with God's purposes and food production was fundamental to the ancient mind. Nothing in nature was thought random or accidental.

By the time of Jesus, grain trading was conducted throughout the Roman Empire on a massive scale. Wheat was preferred in trade, since barley is heavier and therefore more difficult to transport. The farming of barley therefore declined, though its hardiness ensured that a steady local supply could be grown on the poorer soils. Millet was also widely cultivated during the time of Jesus in southern Europe, though it never achieved the popularity of barley or wheat in the Holy Land. (It is mentioned only once in the Bible, as an ingredient of Ezekiel bread.)

Peas and beans

Beans and peas, the pulses, are frequently named in the same sentence with grains in the Bible, and were often accompaniments to grain at the biblical table. They are one of the few vegetables mentioned specifically in the Bible, underscoring their importance as a primary source of vegetable protein and nourishment. Petrified beans were found at the famous excavations of Jarmo in northern Iraq and in the Egyptian tombs at Thebes. Beans were included among the foods forbidden at Passover because they were considered to go through the same leavening process as grain. Ancient Egyptian priests had especially complicated restrictions surrounding the consumption of lentils, peas, favas (broad beans), and chick peas, yet Egyptian royalty were often buried with a supply of beans in their final resting chamber.

Israeli markets are rich in whole grains and beans.

Basic Barley

These six ephahs of barley he gave me; for he said to me, "Do not go empty-handed to your mother-in-law."
Ruth 3:17

Barley is one of the world's hardiest grains and today is used primarily for brewing beer. Native to the Holy Land, it can grow in cold climates, atop mountains, and in unirrigated soil, and is found around the globe in such diverse places as Scotland, the Himalayas, and Korea. Barley has long been known for its easy digestibility. Avoid the pearled barley in favor of the browner, whole-grained varieties generally available in health food stores. However, hulled or hull-less barley will cook faster and taste better than whole barley. Barley and millet are often toasted before boiling water is added to cook them (see next column). Ancient cooking records suggest that roasted barley was made into a brown all-purpose condiment similar to soy sauce.

1 cup (225g) barley (hulled is often sold as Scotch Barley or Pot Barley)

3 cups (900ml) water

Pinch of salt

Rinse barley and place in medium saucepan with water and salt. Bring to a boil, then simmer for 1 hour undisturbed. Barley will expand to three times its dry volume. Serve with butter or gravy in place of rice.
   Yield: About 3 1/2 cups (800g) cooked barley.

Barley Water

This ancient preparation is reputed to clear the complexion and forestall wrinkles, but at the very least it makes a nutritious drink.

1 cup (225g) barley

8 cups (2.4 litres) water

1/2 cup (125g) honey (more if desired)

Pinch of salt

Rinse the barley and place in soup kettle with water and salt. Bring to a boil and simmer a minimum of 2 hours, a maximum of 24 hours, adding more water as necessary to keep water level at about 5 cups (1.4 litres). Longer cooking times will result in a thicker barley water. Strain the barley and discard. Flavor the barley water with honey. Serve chilled.

Basic Millet

Also take for yourself wheat, barley, beans, lentils, millet. . . .
Ezekiel 4:9

Whole millet is a hardy, fiber-rich cereal available at most health food stores. Like barley, it does not contain sufficient gluten to produce yeasted breads, which require wheat. On the other hand, whole millet cooks in 20 to 40 minutes as opposed to the hour needed for barley and the 4 to 6 hours needed for whole wheat kernels. In ancient times, this represented a significant saving in firewood. Millet, a native of Africa, was widely grown in the Roman Empire at the beginning of the Christian era. Its brief popularity was eclipsed by the gains of rice, a less nutritious newcomer from the Orient via Persia.

3/4 cup (175g) hulled millet seed

1 1/2 to 2 cups (450-600ml) boiling water or stock

2 teaspoons oil

1/4 teaspoon salt

Rinse millet seed. Place in saucepan with boiling water or stock and oil and cook over a low flame for 20 minutes, covered. Add salt and let stand another 20 minutes. The seeds will open. Alternatively, toast millet in the oil in a large, heavy skillet until it is lightly browned. Add boiling liquid and proceed as above. Use less liquid for a crisper grain; full amount for a softer grain.
   Yield: About 3 cups (675g) of cooked millet.

Basic Wheat Kernels

Wheat is the queen of grains. Its high gluten content makes it the first choice in fine baking. Indeed, the light, moist, and flaky textures we associate with the best breads and cakes are simply not possible with other flours. The white flour we see every day in the grocery would have been an incomparable luxury to the people of the Bible.

Ancient wheats were such extremely hard-headed, low-yielding little kernels that humanity soon set itself to developing better strains and milling methods, technologies that developed over many centuries. Preparing a pot of whole wheat kernels, or wheat berries as they are often called, will illustrate this property, for even after soaking overnight wheat kernels need 4 to 6 hours of cooking. The homemaker of antiquity often kept a pot of wheat kernels about the fire, soaking, simmering, only occasionally boiling, for 24 hours or more. The thickened milky cooking liquid was taken regularly from this pot (and replenished) to be used in puddings, porridges, sauces, and beverages.

1 cup (225g) whole wheat berries

4 cups (1.2 litres) water

Pinch of salt

In a large saucepan with lid, place wheat berries, water, and salt. Bring to a boil, cover, and simmer 4 to 6 hours or until tender. Add more water as necessary.
   Yield: About 2 3/4 cups (625g) cooked wheat kernels.

Spelt, an ancient wheat, is beginning to be available at health food stores. Spelt cooks faster than wheat kernels without presoaking and has high fiber content with an unusual nutty flavor.

1 cup (225g) spelt

2 1/2 cups (670ml) water

Place in a covered saucepan, bring to boil and then simmer for about 1 1/2 hours until water is absorbed. Let stand 10 minutes.
   Yield: About 3 cups (675g) spelt

Basic Cracked Wheat (Bulgur or Tabbouleh)

. . . So she sat beside the reapers, and he passed parched grain to her; and she ate and was satisfied, and kept some back.
Ruth 2:14

Cracked wheat, bulgur wheat, and tabbouleh refer to whole wheat kernels that have been boiled, dried, and cracked. The cracking of the wheat results in fine, medium, and coarse grains. Thus treated, the wheat will soften quickly when boiling water is added and the grains allowed to soak. The coarser grains may be cooked briefly.

Other grains and even beans may be treated this way, but such products are generally available only in health food stores, while bulgur and tabbouleh are becoming common in supermarkets. To the biblical cook, this process, though initially laborious, resulted in a quick-cooking wheat with better storage properties than the fresh grain. Cracked wheat retains all the fiber of the whole wheat and as a nutritious convenience food has not been surpassed in modern technology. It is sometimes called parched wheat.

1 cup (225g) bulgur wheat

3 cups (900ml) boiling water

Pour boiling water over bulgur wheat and let it stand 30 minutes or until wheat is tender and fluffy. Coarser grains may take longer. Drain if necessary.

Yield: About 21/2 to 3 cups (575-675g) prepared bulgur, ready to eat.

Basic Beans

And Esau said to Jacob, "Please feed me with that stew of red lentils. . . ."
Genesis 25:30 AT

Dry beans are a biblical legacy that have remained in our diet, despite the inroads of canning and freezing. They were used roasted as a snack food, and in soups, stews, salads, and spreads. Chick peas, known also as garbanzos, are the oldest known bean. Fava beans, less common here but long esteemed in the Middle East and in Europe, are also known as horse beans, English beans, or broad beans. Lentils have the great advantage that they do not need soaking, because of their small size. Lentils come in several types: larger brown lentils, standard small ones, and the so-called red lentils, which tempted Esau and which are actually orange in color. Pea beans are dried garden peas.

Roasted Wheat Berries

This ancient cooking method is quick, easy, and provides a crunchy popcornlike food.

1 cup (225g) wheat berries (dried whole wheat grains, available at natural food stores)

1 tablespoon of olive, sesame, or other neutral oil

Salt to taste

Heat a small amount of the oil in a large, heavy frying pan over a fire or a burner on your stove. Add a handful of the dry wheat berries and shake the pan frequently to cook them evenly and to keep them from sticking. When they puff up, they are ready to eat, and you are ready to start a new batch. Sprinkle with salt before serving. Note that the wheat berries will puff up less than popcorn, but will still be quite cooked.

BEAN COOKING CHART (FOR 1 CUP DRY BEANS)

BEAN	SOAKING WATER	SOAKING TIME	COOKING WATER	COOKING TIME	YIELD
Chick Peas	3–4 cups (675–900g)	12–24 hours	4 cups (1.2 litres)	2–3 hours	31/2cups (800g)
Fava Beans (preferably hulled)	4 cups (900g)	24–48 hours	4 cups (1.2 litres)	11/2 hours	21/2 cups (575g)
Lima Beans (use if favas are not available)	4 cups (900g)	overnight	4 cups (1.2 litres)	3/4 hour	21/2 cups (575g)
Lentils (large brown)	3 cups (675g)		3 cups (900ml)	11/2 hours	3 cups (675g)
Lentils (usual small brown)	3 cups (675g)		3 cups (900ml)	3/4 hour	3 cups (675g)
Lentils (red)	3 cups (675g)		3 cups (900ml)	1/2 hour	3 cups (675g)
Pea Beans	3 cups (675g)	overnight	3 cups (900ml)	11/2–2 hours	2 cups (450g)

General rules for all beans: Change the soaking water several times, if possible, since this will make them more digestible. Using the longer soaking time will mean less cooking time. Never add salt during cooking as then the beans will not soften, but add after cooking, if salt is desired. Bring to boil in cooking water, cover, and then simmer.

Cooking times are approximate, so check for doneness. While lentils generally do not require soaking, they vary in size and degree of hardness (especially if bought in health food stores), so check directions before deciding on soaking and allow for additional cooking time, if needed.

Roasted Wheat Berries (top left), Basic Cracked Wheat (right), and Bulgur, or Cracked Wheat Pilaf (bottom).

Bulgur or Cracked Wheat Pilaf

1 cup (225g) bulgur or cracked wheat (coarse grains are best for pilaf)

1 to 3 teaspoons spices (cumin, coriander seed, minced (finely chopped) garlic, ground pomegranate seed, dried thyme) (optional)

2 tablespoons butter

2 cups (600ml) water or stock (chicken, beef, lamb, or vegetable)

Salt to taste

Parsley

Coriander leaves

Sauté grain and spices in butter for 3 minutes. Add stock or water. Bring to a boil, cover, reduce heat, and simmer for 10 minutes. Turn off heat and let pilaf sit for 15 minutes. Salt to taste. Fluff with fork and garnish with greens. Serve with meat, chicken, or fish.

Cream of Barley Soup

. . . Now they came to Bethlehem at the beginning of barley harvest.
Ruth 1:22

Ruth and Naomi availed themselves of the ancient charity that allowed the poor to glean the barley fields after reaping.

3/4 cup (175g) barley

5 cups (1.4 litres) vegetable, beef, or chicken stock or bouillon cubes*

1/2 cup (150ml) heavy (double) cream

Salt to taste

1/4 cup (50g) celery leaves

Fresh parsley or coriander leaves

Wash the barley in warm water. Cook in 4 cups (1.2 litres) of the stock with celery leaves for 2½ hours. Mash the cooked barley by hand (avoid using a blender or food processor, as this tends to create a gummy texture). Add the remaining cup of stock. Before serving, heat barley and add the cream. Salt to taste. Garnish with parsley or coriander leaves.

This dish depends on a good stock to give it definition. Bouillon cubes are a last resort if fresh stock is unavailable.

Barley Herb Soup

Simmered barley herb broth was a health tonic to the ancients, taken for upset stomachs, fevers, and post-festival hangovers.

1/2 cup (125g) barley

4 cups (1.2 litres) vegetable or chicken stock

1 to 4 tablespoons of fresh or dried herbs (thyme, pennyroyal†, parsley, celery leaves, coriander leaves, savory, chervil, mint)*

1 onion, chopped

3 tablespoons chopped celery

2 tablespoons butter or oil

Salt to taste

Rinse the barley and put into a soup pot with the stock. Add the herbs. Bring to a boil, then simmer gently for 5 hours. Remove scum from the broth as it surfaces. Add water as necessary. Sauté the onion and celery in butter until brown and caramelized. Add to soup pot. Salt to taste and garnish with fresh herbs.

1 tablespoon fresh herb = 1 teaspoon dried

† Pennyroyal contains an oil which can cause abortion.

Vegetable Soup With Whole Grains

When Daniel was a captive in the Babylonian court of King Nebuchadnezzar, he asked to be given a vegetarian diet so as to avoid the rich food and non-kosher meat. The king's stewards were afraid they would be blamed if Daniel became weak. To reassure them, Daniel and his three Hebrew companions conducted an experiment for 10 days, eating only vegetables. *"And at the end of ten days their countenance appeared better and fatter in flesh than all the young men who ate the portion of the king's delicacies"* (Daniel 1:8–16).

4 tablespoons butter or vegetable oil

4 carrots, chopped

3 onions, chopped

2 parsnips, chopped

2 stalks celery, chopped

2 quarts (2.4 litres) water or stock

1 cup (225g) barley, millet, or bulgur wheat

1 teaspoon salt

1/2 pound (225g) beet greens, spinach, or red lettuce leaves

1 cup cooked chick peas

Chopped parsley and/or coriander leaves

In a large soup pot, sauté the chopped vegetables in the butter or oil until lightly cooked. Add the water. Add the barley, millet, or bulgur. Add salt. Simmer for at least 1 hour or until grain is tender. During the last 15 minutes of cooking, add the chick peas and shred the washed greens into the soup. Garnish with parsley and/or coriander leaves.

Cold Grain and Bean Salads

A land of wheat and barley. . . .
Deuteronomy 8:8

3 cups (675g) freshly cooked warm barley, bulgur wheat, whole wheat kernels, or millet (see Basic Recipes, pages 21, 22) or

3 cups (675g) freshly cooked warm lentils, chick peas, or fava beans (broad beans). See page 22 for Basic Recipes.

SALAD

1/2 cup (125g) parsley *and/or* coriander leaves, chopped

1 bunch scallions (spring onions), chopped

2 cucumbers, chopped

1 bulb fennel, chopped, or 4 stalks celery, chopped

1 bunch radishes, chopped

1/2 cup (125g) pitted black olives

1/2 cup (125g) white raisins (sultanas) or date pieces

3 hard-boiled eggs, sliced (optional)

DRESSING

1 clove garlic (optional)

1 heaping tablespoon horseradish mustard

1 to 2 teaspoons honey

2 tablespoons fresh herbs (such as dill, thyme, oregano, mint, chives, savory, and chervil)

1 tablespoon cumin

1/2 cup (150ml) olive oil

1/4 cup (75ml) vinegar, tart grape juice, or lemon juice (more if desired)

Salt to taste

Garnishes (optional): Poppy or sesame seeds, crumbled goat cheese, romaine (cos) lettuce, fresh coriander, chopped

Rub a large salad bowl with the cut clove of garlic and discard. In the salad bowl, prepare the dressing. Mix mustard, honey, herbs, and spices. Add oil, then add vinegar or tart juice, varying proportions as desired. Salt to taste. Mix warm grains or beans with dressing. Allow to cool. Add salad ingredients and toss. Chill if desired. Garnish with poppy or sesame seed, goat cheese, or romaine (cos) lettuce. Proportions can be varied to taste. These salads are a meal in themselves as well as excellent snacks and side dishes.

Barley Stew With Lentils

Whole grains and beans, eaten together, were a primary source of complete protein, B vitamins, and dietary fiber for the people of the Holy Land. Since modern nutritional science affirms the health value of these foods, serve them with confidence any time of day.

1/3 cup (85g) chopped onions

1/2 cup (125g) chopped celery

1/2 cup (125g) chopped carrots

5 tablespoons butter

5 cups (1.4 litres) water or stock

1 cup (225g) dried lentils, picked over and washed

1/2 cup (125g) barley

1/8 teaspoon rosemary

2 teaspoons salt

2 teaspoons ground cumin

1/2 pound (225g) beet greens or spinach

In a large soup pot, sauté the chopped onion, celery, and carrots in the butter. Add the water or stock, lentils, barley, rosemary, salt, and cumin. Bring to a boil, turn down heat, and cook until lentils and barley are tender, about 1 hour. Remove scum as it forms. Add greens for the last 15 minutes of cooking.

Barley Stew With Lentils.

Tabbouleh Salad

So the children of Israel camped in Gilgal, and kept the Passover on the fourteenth day of the month at twilight on the plains of Jericho. And they ate of the produce of the land on the day after the Passover, unleavened bread and parched grain, on the very same day.
Joshua 5:10, 11

1 cup (225g) fine-grained bulgur wheat

3 cups (900ml) boiling water

1 bunch scallions (spring onions), finely chopped

2 cups (900g) parsley, chopped

4 tablespoons vinegar (lemon juice can be substituted)

1/2 cup (125g) chopped radishes

Salt to taste

3 tablespoons olive oil

1 teaspoon sharp prepared mustard

Romaine (cos) lettuce leaves

1/4 cup (50g) fresh mint leaves, finely chopped (optional)

In a large bowl, cover the bulgur wheat with boiling water. Let soak for 30 minutes or until tender. Drain the wheat and combine with all other ingredients except lettuce leaves. Marinate and chill for several hours, or overnight, in refrigerator. Heap salad on a platter and arrange lettuce leaves around it so that they may be used as scoops. This is an excellent luncheon dish.

Esau's Pottage

Esau's Pottage is one of the most famous recipes in history, and to this day various simmered red-lentil dishes are known as Esau's Pottage in the Bible lands. Esau, like his father, Isaac, was susceptible to the blandishments of a well-prepared stew. The improvident Esau is victimized by the manipulation of his brother and mother in Genesis, chapters 25–27.

1 onion, chopped

1 tablespoon olive oil

1/2 teaspoon ground cumin

1/2 teaspoon ground coriander

2 cloves garlic, minced (chopped finely)

3 cups (900ml) beef or vegetable stock, or water mixed with beef or vegetable bouillon cubes

1 cup (225g) red lentils

1/2 pound (225g) spinach or young sorrel leaves, shredded (optional)

Salt to taste

In a large stewing pot, sauté the chopped onion in the olive oil with the cumin and coriander. Add the garlic at the last moment and brown. Add lentils and stock. Stir well and bring to a boil. Reduce heat. Simmer 25–35 minutes or until lentils are tender. Add spinach 5–10 minutes before serving. Salt to taste. Serves 6 as a side dish; double quantities to serve as a main dish.

Saffron Pilaf

Spikenard and saffron,
Calamus and cinnamon . . .
Myrrh and aloes,
With all the chief spices.
Song of Solomon 4:14

Zest of one orange

2 cups (600ml) boiling water

1 teaspoon saffron threads

2 tablespoons warm water

3 tablespoons oil

1 medium onion, sliced

1/2 teaspoonful each ground cumin, ground coriander, ground cinnamon (more cumin and coriander if desired)

1/4 cup (50g) pine nuts

1/2 cup (125g) white raisins (sultanas)— optional

1/2 cup (150ml) extra water (optional— only if using raisins)

3/4 cups (175g) dry hulled millet and 2 1/2 cups (750ml) water *or*

1 cup (225g) dry hulled barley and 3 cups (900ml) water *or*

1 cup (225g) dry bulgur and 3 cups (900ml) water

A few hours before cooking, place saffron threads in warm water and leave to soak. The threads will soften and color the water orange. When ready to start, peel outside skin of orange (zest) and cut peel into small slivers. Put in bowl and pour in 1 cup of boiling water. Let sit for 5 minutes. Drain and repeat. Set aside.

In a skillet, heat oil and sauté the onion until transparent. Add the cumin, coriander, and cinnamon and sauté briefly. Add the orange zest, the pine nuts, and the dry grain. Sauté, stirring steadily until the grains are coated with oil. Add a little more oil if needed. Then add the cooking water, the saffron water, and the raisins (sultanas) with their extra liquid if using them. Bring to a boil, turn down to simmer, cover, and cook as follows:

Millet: Cook for 40 minutes, let rest in covered pot 15 minutes

Barley: Cook for 1 hour

Bulgur: Cook for 1/2 hour, let rest in covered pot for 15 minutes

Note that cooking times are approximate; check for doneness.

Whole Grains With Goat Cheese and Chick Peas

. . . earthen vessels and wheat, barley and flour, parched grain and beans, lentils and parched seeds, honey and curds, sheep and cheese of the herd, for David and the people who were with him to eat. . . .
2 Samuel 17:28, 29

1/2 cup (150ml) olive oil

1 teaspoon sharp prepared mustard

1/3 cup (70ml) fresh lemon juice or vinegar

Salt and pepper to taste

3 cups (675g) softened bulgur or cooked barley, millet, or wheat kernels (see Basic Recipes, pages 21–22)

1/2 cup (125g) parsley, chopped

1/2 cup (125g) fresh mint leaves (or to taste)

1 bunch green onions (spring onion tops), chopped

2 cups (450g) cooked chick peas (16-ounce can)

4 ounces (125g) feta cheese, chopped into chunks

2 tablespoons chopped black olives

Lettuce leaves

Whisk olive oil, mustard, and vinegar or lemon juice into a dressing. In a salad bowl, combine grains, parsley, mint, green onions, chick peas, cheese, and olives. Add dressing. Season with salt and pepper. Let marinate and chill overnight if possible. Arrange lettuce leaves so they can be used as scoops. Serve with grapes and unleavened barley bread.

Chick Pea Wheat Soup

This hearty porridge was a typical breakfast food in the ancient Holy Land. It is traditionally served on Saint Lucy's Day, December 13.

1/2 cup (125g) dried chick peas or 1 cup (225g) cooked chick peas (canned may be used)

1 cup (225g) whole wheat kernels

1 bay leaf

1/4 teaspoon cinnamon (more if desired)

1 to 2 teaspoons salt

8 cups (2.4 litres) water

Honey to taste

Soak the dried chick peas and wheat kernels overnight in separate containers. In a soup pot, place the drained wheat kernels, bay leaf, cinnamon, salt, and approximately 8 cups (2.4 litres) of fresh water. Bring to a boil, then simmer for 2 hours. Add the soaked chick peas and continue simmering for 1 to 2 hours or until the wheat is tender. (Canned chick peas should be added to the simmering wheat after 3 hours). Add more water as necessary. Serve with honey.

Saffron Pilaf.

Kibbeh (Ground Lamb With Bulgur)

Thus they shall prepare the lamb, the grain offering, and the oil. . . .
Ezekiel 46:15

Kibbeh has been the "hamburger" of the Holy Land for millennia. The whole-grain bulgur not only extends the meat, but also adds fiber and crunchy texture.

2 cups (450g) bulgur wheat

5 cups (1.4 litres) boiling water

1 pound (450g) ground (minced) lamb (ground beef may be used)

2 teaspoons cumin

1 onion, minced (very finely chopped)

Salt and pepper to taste

Oil for frying

Soak the bulgur in the boiling water. Let sit for about 30 minutes or until water is absorbed. Squeeze out excess water with hands or a towel. Mix with lamb, cumin, onion, salt, and pepper.

To bake: Spread mixture on a shallow, oiled baking pan and score the top with a knife diagonally to make diamond-shaped portions. Bake in a moderate oven (350°F, 180°C, Gas mark 4) for about 25 minutes or until a knife inserted into meat comes out clean. Place under broiler (grill) to brown the top.

To fry: Form patties, like hamburgers, or into oblongs like thick fingers, adding 1-2 eggs beaten. Put in refrigerator for about an hour. Fry in hot oil, turning on all sides to form a good crust.

Serve with Whole Wheat Sourdough Bread, Yogurt and Sesame Sauce, grilled leeks and scallions (spring onions), lettuce, and radishes.

Vegetarian Kibbeh

In place of meat, substitute:

1/2 cup (125g) cooked lentils

1/4 cup (70ml) olive oil

2 eggs, beaten

Proceed as above.

Fresh Fava Beans With Ground Lamb (Mefarka)

Mefarka is a Middle Eastern chili—chopped meat, beans, and spices, including cumin (a Holy Land native also popular with Mexican cooks).

3 pounds (1.4kg) fresh unshelled fava (broad) beans or 1 pound (450g) frozen

2 quarts (2.4 litres) water

2 tablespoons olive oil

1 pound (450g) ground (minced) lamb

1 teaspoon dried thyme or 2 teaspoons fresh

1/2 teaspoon cumin

1/2 teaspoon coriander

1/2 teaspoon cinnamon

1/2 teaspoon dried mint or 1 teaspoon fresh

2 eggs, beaten

2 teaspoons salt

1 tablespoon black cumin seed (optional)

Shell fresh fava (broad) beans. In a large pot with a vented lid, simmer the fresh or frozen fava beans in 1/2 cup (150ml) water and 2 tablespoons olive oil for 30 minutes to an hour or until tender. Add more water as it evaporates, but keep water level low. In a large skillet, boil the ground (minced) lamb in 1 cup (300ml) water for 5 minutes. Pour off this water, which will contain much of the excess fat. Return skillet to the heat and let lamb begin to fry in the remaining fat. Stir in the spices and herbs except for the black cumin. Continue frying for abut 10 minutes until texture is dry. Mash cooked fava beans into cooked lamb. Add beaten eggs and stir until eggs are set. Add salt and garnish with black cumin seed. Serve with a salad of orange sections and fresh mint leaves, olives, cheese, and Whole Wheat Sourdough Bread.

Three Bean Soup

1 large onion or leek, chopped

1 clove garlic, mashed

2 celery stalks with leaves, chopped

1 tablespoon olive oil

1/2 teaspoon cumin

1/2 teaspoon coriander

1 bay leaf

1/2 teaspoon thyme

1 handful parsley, chopped

1/2 cup (125g) dry fava (broad) beans soaked in water for 48 hours

1/4 cup (50g) dry chick peas, soaked in water for 24 hours

6 cups (1.8 litres) water

1/4 cup (50g) dry lentils

1/4 cup (50g) pearl barley

Salt and pepper to taste

In a large soup pot, sauté onions, garlic, and celery in olive oil. Add herbs (reserve some parsley for garnish) and spices except salt and continue to sauté for 5 minutes. Add fava (broad) beans, chick peas, and water. Cook for 1 hour. Add barley and lentils and cook for another hour or until tender. Garnish with parsley. Salt and pepper to taste before serving. This soup can be served hot or cold. It keeps well and can be frozen.

Opposite: Kibbeh (Ground Lamb With Bulgur), with Grilled Leeks and Scallions (see p.72).

Traditional Sabbath Casserole

Remember the Sabbath day, to keep it holy. Six days you shall labor and do all your work, but the seventh day is the Sabbath of the Lord your God. In it you shall do no work: you, nor your son, nor your daughter, nor your manservant, nor your maidservant, nor your cattle, nor your stranger who is within your gates.
Exodus 20:8–10

The Fourth Commandment forbade all labor on the Sabbath, including cooking and housework. Before sundown on the Sabbath, casseroles were placed in the embers of the Sabbath fire to bake overnight, providing a hearty one-dish meal for the day of rest. Records of this type of cooking date as far back as the Second Temple, about the time of Jesus.

2 cups (450g) dried hulled fava (broad) beans or other dry white beans

3 onions, diced

3 pounds (1.4kg) brisket or lamb shanks

3 tablespoons olive oil

2 teaspoons ground cumin

2 teaspoons ground coriander

2 cloves garlic, crushed

2 teaspoons salt

1 cup (225g) barley

2 tablespoons whole wheat flour

1 teaspoon capers

1 tablespoon chopped olives

2 tablespoons raisins

6 cups (1.8 litres) boiling water (approximately)

Soak the fava (broad) beans for 1 to 2 days. Other dry white beans need only be soaked overnight. In a Dutch oven, brown the onions and meat in olive oil. Sprinkle on the spices and salt, stirring as the onions brown. Stir in all other ingredients except the water. Pour in enough boiling water to rise an inch (21/2cm) above mixture. Cover tightly with lid. Bake for 24 hours in an oven at 250ºF (120ºC, Gas mark 1/2) or 4 to 5 hours at 350ºF (180ºC, Gas mark 4). Serve with fresh fruit, a salad, and Pistachio Almond Cookies.

Lentil Pancakes

. . . there was a piece of ground full of lentils. . . .
2 Samuel 23:11

This ancient cooking method of drying and grinding beans into flour works with chick peas and fava (broad) beans also.

1 cup (225g) lentils

3 eggs

1/4 cup ((50g) honey

Olive or sesame oil

Spread lentils on an ungreased pie plate or baking sheet and roast in a moderate (300ºF, 150ºC, Gas mark 2) oven for 20 minutes. Lentils should be completely dried out and easy to grind. Grind lentils with a nut or coffee grinder, or mortar and pestle until they are powdered into the texture of flour. Set aside.

   In a large bowl, beat the eggs. Add the honey. Mix well and add the ground lentils, blending thoroughly into a batter. Oil a griddle or large pan and cook like pancakes. Serve with Tabbouleh Salad, steamed vegetables, or as a sweet with Grape Honey or date syrup.

Pan-Roasted Chick Peas

One of the earliest beans cultivated, chick peas were a staple in the ancient Holy Land. This ancient cooking method provided Imperial Rome with its favorite street food. Beans prepared this way make a quick wholesome snack food.

1 to 2 cups (225-450g) dried chick peas

3 cups (900ml) water

Cumin to taste

Salt to taste (optional)

Soak chick peas overnight in the water. Change the water a few times if possible. The next day, dry the chick peas on a plate in the sun or in a low oven (250ºF, 120ºC, Gas mark 1/2). Heat in a large, heavy frying pan on the hot coals, or on the stove. Shake the pan frequently to cook them evenly and keep them from burning. When a batch is lightly browned (taste to check if done), transfer to a bowl and sprinkle with cumin or salt. Continue until finished. The roasted chick peas will be chewy, with a taste and texture much like hot chestnuts. Note that soaked chick peas can be kept in the freezer for future use.

Bread

Your threshing shall last till the time of vintage, and the vintage shall last till the time of sowing; you shall eat your bread to the full, and dwell in your land safely.
Leviticus 26:5

Bread is mentioned hundreds of times in the Bible, more times than any other food. The word can refer generally to all food, but most often it means the loaves, cakes, and biscuits we commonly recognize as bread. The Bible records many instances of brethren eating bread together, of a stranger being given bread, and of God providing bread to His people. Jesus describes Himself as the Bread of Life (John 6:35).

Unleavened bread
The first breads of the Bible were unleavened. Similar to soft tortillas when hot, they cool into crackers and crisp breads. Barley, the most plentiful grain of the Holy Land, was the chief flour. Barley produces more grain per acre and requires less water than wheat. However, it lacks the abundant gluten of wheat. Gluten is a protein that allows for the enzymatic action of yeast. Two primitive wheats, emmer and einkorn, grew alongside barley. Many centuries of refinement in Egypt, Mesopotamia, and Rome were necessary to produce the bread wheats we know today.

Barley cakes are specifically mentioned in the Scriptures as an integral part of the diet of the early Hebrews. The Feast of Unleavened Bread was an ancient barley harvest festival that became part of Passover (Leviticus 23:6). In Judges 7:13, Gideon dreams of a barley cake that rolls through the camp of a besieging enemy, knocking down their tents. If you ever have day-old leftovers of unleavened barley cake, this story will seem less fantastic. Barley loaves were distributed by Jesus and the Disciples (John 6:9–13), the original loaves and fishes.

The yearly flooding of the Nile Valley enabled the regular cultivation of wheat. The baking skills of the early Hebrews were expanded by their sojourn in Egypt, for the Egyptians developed the technology of natural yeasts and its applications in leavening bread and brewing beer. A mixture of wheat flour and water left to sit in a warm place for a few days will ferment, developing the yeasts that cause bread dough to rise. We are familiar with this process in the making of sourdough bread. Warmth and timing are key factors in its success. Natural leavening, or sourdough starter, traps air within the bread, producing a lighter, larger-volume loaf than one made with the same amount of unleavened flour.

Egyptian breads
Ancient papyri record over thirty different Egyptian breads. Stone carvings from the Egyptian tombs show loaves shaped to look like cows and birds, and coiled into spiral snakes. Triangular breads were stacked against each other on racks and small rolls were offered to the gods, two hundred at a time.

The Hebrews did not entirely trust this process of leavening learned from their Egyptian taskmasters (Exodus 12:15). They considered the heaviness of unleavened bread a sign of its purity and wholesomeness; the lightness of leavened bread was a trickery, a sign of corruption. This concept endured in the early Christian writings (1 Corinthians 5:7 and Matthew 16:6).

Unleavened breads of wheat and barley, sometimes referred to as show-breads in the Bible, remained important for ceremonial offerings. Most Bible readers are familiar with the story of the Hebrews fleeing Egypt in such haste that their bread could not be leavened (Exodus 12:34). The matzoh of Passover commemorates this liberation. The ancient preference for unleavened bread was recorded in stone on the Roman Arch of Titus, built after the conquest of the Holy Land, which depicted captive Hebrews forced to present their showbread as a tribute to the emperor. The communion wafer is a latter-day descendant of the traditional unleavened breads.

First ovens
The first baking ovens were portable clay cylinders, much like oversize jars. A fire was made in the bottom of the oven. When it had burned down, the ashes were swept out and the bread placed on the cylinder walls to bake by the retained heat. This method was a substantial improvement over the one that preceded it, the baking of bread on flat stones at the edge of the fires. Baking is one culinary technology particularly amenable to specialization, and large-scale baking became necessary in Egypt to feed the laborers of long-term projects such as the building of pyramids. In Mesopotamia, bakeries were connected to the temples, physically and psychologically. The ancient Hebrew state also developed large-scale, professional bakeries. The production of the Sabbath bread was taken over by one family in Jerusalem.

Arab women make bread by traditional methods in northern Israel.

Preparing Naturally Leavened Bread (Sourdough)

Sourdough baking requires three stages of leavening flour and water by natural yeasts. These stages are the starter, the sponge, and the dough. A few days are needed to swing into full production, but once organized, one can easily turn out delicious breads and cakes.

Step One
The first step is to make the *starter*. Combine 2 cups (450g) of flour and 2 cups (600ml) of water in a glass or ceramic bowl with a wooden spoon. Let sit uncovered for 2 to 5 days in a warm place, stirring occasionally. The mixture needs contact with the air so that invisible airborne yeasts can enter it. The yeasts cause the release of gases, changing the volume and texture of the mixture. When ready, the flour and water will have a clean, yeasty smell and small bubbles, and will be stickier than the original paste. This is sourdough starter and it is ready to leaven breads and cakes. Should contamination occur, off-colors like orange or blue will appear and a disagreeable odor will be exuded. Discard, scald bowl, and start again.

Step Two
The second step is to make the *sponge*. Add 2 cups (450g) of whole wheat flour and 2 cups (600ml) of warm water to the starter. (These amounts may be increased in specific recipes.) Blend well. Cover and let sit for 8 to 10 hours or overnight in a warm spot. The resulting sponge will double in volume and seem sticky like the starter. Take 1 cup (225g) of sponge and keep aside in a cool place. After a day or two, the reserved sponge becomes the starter for the next baking.

Step Three
The third step is to make the *dough*. Add 3 cups (675g) of flour and 1 to 2 cups (300-600ml) of water to the sponge along with the eggs, milk, honey, or oil called for in a specific recipe. Blend these ingredients and turn onto a floured board for kneading. Knead for a minimum of 10 minutes, then return dough to bowl. Cover and let sit in a warm place for 2 to 4 hours. The dough will double in volume. This is called rising or proofing. After the first rising, the leavened dough is turned back onto a floured board and shaped into loaves, rolls, and cakes. The shaped loaves are left to rise for 1 to 2 hours. A loaf of sourdough bread is generally baked for an hour at 350°F (180°C, Gas mark 4). Higher temperatures produce a chewier crust.

The warmth of your kitchen will determine the exact times necessary to produce sourdough starter, sponge, and dough. Times may vary as much as 24 hours, so the above directions are meant only as a general guide. You may prefer your sourdough quite sour and wish to allow extra time in each phase of starter, sponge, and dough.

Starter should never be stored in a tightly closed container, as the gases can build up and cause a small explosion. Starter may be kept in the refrigerator, but will require a few wakeup hours at room temperature before use. If the original starter is not regularly used to make sponge, it will become very sour and should be refreshed weekly with 1 cup (225g) flour and 1 cup (300ml) warm water.

The ancient storage method for starter was to dry it into a hard nugget, and this is still the best way if starter will not be used for a few weeks. Let a cup (225g) of sponge dry at room temperature (sunlight speeds the process) into a hard, dry lump. Dried starter is reconstituted by soaking in water for 3 to 12 hours: Keep the dry lump underwater by inverting a dish on top of the container in which it is soaking.

The principles of sourdough baking are those used in the production of any fermented product. Yogurt, wine, and penicillin are made the same way. The natural, healthy yeast is nurtured through warmth, regulation, and adequate food supply. Extremes in temperature such as freezing and baking retard and ultimately kill the yeasts. This is why only warm water is added to the different phases and why baking ingredients should be at room temperature. The yeasts of sourdough baking are among nature's most resilient fungi. Starters have been known to be in continuous use for 80 years.

Sarah's Bread

Abraham hastened into the tent to Sarah and said, "Quickly, make ready three measures of fine meal; knead it and make cakes."
Genesis 18:6

This occasion of hospitality is the first biblical reference to baking. Fine meal means wheat flour, not the more common barley, and 3 measures is approximately 28 cups (10.5kg). Hence, Abraham directs that the finest provisions of the household be offered to his guests. The Patriarchal family included numerous servants, retainers, relatives, and their children. As there were only three guests, the lavish amount of flour suggests that the entire household would share in the meal.

3 1/2 cups (400g) whole wheat flour plus extra for flouring boards

1 teaspoon salt

3/4 cup (220ml) lukewarm water

Sesame or vegetable oil

Sift together flour and salt. Add the water and mix with a wooden spoon into a smooth paste. Turn onto a floured board and knead at least 10 minutes. Put dough in a bowl and cover with a damp cloth. Let sit in a warm place for 1 to 3 hours. Divide the dough into 8 pieces and form into balls. On the floured board, roll each piece into a flat circle about 6 inches (15cm) across. Cover these pieces with the damp cloth and let sit for 30 minutes. Cook each bread individually in a lightly oiled frying pan or bake several pieces at 500°F (250°C, Gas mark 9) until the edges curl up. The adventurous may use large flat stones or oiled, unglazed tiles at the side of a fireplace or outdoor barbecue grill. The object here is to get the bread as close to the heat as possible without burning it in the fire.

Matzoh, the Unleavened Bread

They baked unleavened cakes of the dough which they had brought out of Egypt; for it was not leavened, because they were driven out of Egypt and could not wait. . . .
Exodus 12:39

Unleavened bread is considered the "bread of affliction" and is the only bread permitted to Jews during the week of Passover.* It is easy to make, and many people find it extremely tasty.

2 cups (450g) whole wheat flour *or*

1 cup (225g) whole wheat flour and 1 cup (225g) barley flour

3/4 cup (220ml) water

Combine flour and water thoroughly with wooden spoon. Dust the top of this mixture with a small amount of flour. Flour hands and knead the dough lightly for 3 minutes. Divide into 6 to 8 balls, rounding them with floured hands. (Cracker-size matzoh can be made with smaller balls of dough.) Oil a cookie sheet or use a heavy one that does not require oiling. Place balls on cookie sheet. Press down each ball with hands to make a flat cracker about 5 inches (130mm) in diameter. Or use a rolling pin to flatten. Prick with a fork, to prevent swelling. Bake for 10 minutes in a hot, preheated oven (500°F, 250°C, Gas mark 9). Remove matzohs and serve soon if they are to be eaten soft. Otherwise, turn off the oven and leave the matzohs in until the oven is cool. They will now have the consistency of crisp bread and can be stored in airtight canisters for long periods. Serve with soups and cheese spreads.

* To qualify for Passover use today, no more than 17 minutes may elapse from the time the flour is moistened, the matzoh mixed, kneaded, and placed in the oven.

Matzoh, the Unleavened Bread.

Barley Cakes

And you shalt eat it as barley cakes. . . .
Ezekiel 4:12

1 1/2 cups (450ml) hot milk

1/4 teaspoon salt

3 tablespoons honey

3 cups (675g) barley flour

3/4 cup (175g) raisins

Oil for frying

Combine all ingredients and shape into balls. Flatten into rounds. Fry in hot oil 5 minutes on each side or bake 20 to 25 minutes in a preheated oven at 400°F (200°C, Gas mark 6). Serve with Ur, Green Butter Herb Cheese.

Whole Wheat Sourdough Bread

Our familiar whole wheat loaf was a luxury to the working people of the Bible. They generally mixed the cheaper barley and wheat flour together, as in the variation on the right. This master recipe can be used for loaves, flat breads, pitas, and rolls.

The evening before baking, prepare the sponge:

1 cup (225g) sourdough starter

2 cups (450g) whole wheat flour

2 cups (600ml) warm water

Mix together in a wooden or plastic bowl (avoid metal) and let sit overnight in a warm place. Remove 1 cup of sponge and set aside to be used as starter in the future. The next day, prepare the dough as follows:

6 cups (1.4kg) whole wheat flour plus 1 cup for kneading

2 cups (600ml) warm water

2 teaspoons salt

2 tablespoons honey

2 tablespoons vegetable oil

Sesame seed or black cumin

Combine flour, water, salt, and honey with sponge into a smooth dough and turn onto a floured board. Knead with floured hands for 10 minutes or 300 times, adding more flour if necessary to keep dough stiff and surfaces floured. If you are kneading with a food processor, use only 5 1/2 cups (1.1kg) flour. Process for 30 seconds until a ball of dough forms. Place kneaded dough in bowl, brush top with vegetable oil, and cover. Allow to rise for 3 hours or a little longer in a warm place.

Reknead briefly and shape into 2 loaves. Let sit in a warm place for another 2 hours. Slit the tops, so loaves will not crack while baking. Brush tops with water occasionally to retain moisture. Preheat oven to 350°F (180°C, Gas mark 4) and bake about 1 hour. Test for doneness by inserting a knife. If bread is done, the knife will come out dry. If bread is undercooked,

check after 10 minutes. Allow the bread to sit at least 10 minutes before serving or slicing.

SHAPED ROLLS
After allowing dough to rise for 3 hours, reknead briefly and divide into 16 pieces. Make snakes or spirals by rolling dough with hand into thin ropes on a floured surface. Braid, coil, or attach ends for circlets. Shape into triangles. Place on a baking sheet and let rise for an hour. Sprinkle with sesame seed or black cumin if desired. Preheat oven to 450°F (230°C, Gas mark 8). Bake 10 to 15 minutes.

PITAS OR POCKET BREADS
Divide dough into 16 small balls. Shape each piece into a ball on a floured surface or between palms. Cover to keep off drafts and let sit in warm place for 10 to 20 minutes. Preheat oven to 450°F (230°C, Gas mark 8). Roll out with a rolling pin on a floured surface, turning pin to make a circle between 1/8 and 1/4 inch (3–5mm) thick. The rounds must be evenly flat to make a pocket. Place on unoiled baking sheets and bake 10 minutes.

BREAD BAKED IN A CLAY POT
In ancient times, a wet clay pot was started at the edge of the fire and moved into the hot coals gradually, so that the clay would not break. A small clay pot with a cover, approximately 6 by 9 inches (15 by 23cm), works well for a single loaf of bread. Cut the above recipe by half. Soak the bottom section of the pot in water for 15 minutes before shaping the dough and putting it into the soaked pot for the last rising. Do not grease the pot. Fifteen minutes before baking, soak the clay top in water. Cover the bread and put in a cold oven which you turn immediately to 475°F (240°C, Gas mark 9). Bake for 45 minutes, taking the cover off for the last 10 minutes to brown the top. Test by inserting a knife. If it comes out dry, bread is done.

Barley Wheat Sourdough Bread

Then a man came from Baal Shalisha, and brought the man of God bread of the firstfruits, twenty loaves of barley bread, and newly ripened grain in his knapsack. And he said, "Give it to the people, that they may eat."
2 Kings 4:42

Prepare Whole Wheat Sourdough Bread, substituting for the 6 cups (1.4kg) of whole wheat flour in the dough:

2 cups (450g) barley flour

4 cups (900g) whole wheat flour

1 extra cup (225g) either flour for kneading

Date Nut Bread

Jericho, famous for its dates, was called the city of palms, in reference to its date trees. This ancient-style recipe is naturally rich and moist and needs no milk or eggs.

2 cups (450g) naturally leavened sponge (see page 33)

4 cups (900g) whole wheat flour

2 cups (600ml) warm water

2 cups (450g) dried dates, chopped

1 teaspoon salt

2 tablespoons date syrup or honey

4 tablespoons vegetable oil

1/2 to 1 cup (50–125g) chopped walnuts

To the naturally leavened sponge add the rest of the ingredients and mix well. Turn the dough onto a floured board. Knead for 10 minutes. Add more flour and water as necessary to achieve the right texture (on the dry side). Divide into 2 loaves and place on oiled baking pans. Place the loaves in a warm spot, gently covered. Allow to rise for 2 to 3 hours. Slit the tops with a knife and brush the loaves with water. Bake in a moderately hot oven (375°F, 190°C, Gas mark 5) for an hour. Brush the tops with water once

Whole Wheat Sourdough Bread (top) and Date Nut Bread (bottom).

or twice while baking to conserve moisture. Cool in the pan for 10 minutes before removing.

As with many sourdough breads, this one is even better a day or two after baking. Date Nut Bread, a mild white cheese, olives, and mint tea make a perfect light lunch.

Sourdough Fig Roll

And they gave him a piece of a cake of figs and two clusters of raisins. So when he had eaten, his strength came back to him. . . .
1 Samuel 30:12

2 cups (600ml) warm water

2 cups (450g) sponge (see page 33)

2 cups (450g) whole wheat flour plus extra for kneading

1 teaspoon salt

3 tablespoons honey

1 teaspoon cinnamon

3 tablespoons vegetable oil

1 cup (225g) fig preserves *or* chopped dry figs

1/4 cup (50g) sesame seed (optional)

Combined sponge and warm water. Add flour, salt, honey, cinnamon, and oil. Knead the dough for 10 minutes to a smooth, dry texture on a floured board. Add small amounts of flour or water if necessary. With a floured rolling pin, roll dough into a square or rectangle about 1/2 inch (15mm) thick. Spread the fig preserves over the rolled dough and sprinkle with the sesame seed. Roll up into a cylinder. Slit the top with a knife, place in a greased baking pan, and let sit for 1 to 3 hours, depending on the warmth of the kitchen. Brush tops with water during the rising and baking. Bake in a preheated often at 350°F (180°C, Gas mark 4)for 1 hour.

For individual fig cakes: When cylindrical loaf has been rolled up, cut into thick slices. Lay these slices on greased baking sheet and let rise for an hour. Bake the fig cakes for 20 minutes in an oven preheated to 350°F (180°C, Gas mark 4).

Sabbath Bread or Challah

For the Sabbath, each family prepares 2 loaves of bread to recall the double portion of Sabbath manna provided by God in the desert (Exodus 16:22). The preparation of Sabbath bread became quite elaborate in ancient Jerusalem and was eventually handled by professional bakers.

5 eggs

1 tablespoon salt

1/2 cup (125g) honey

8 cups (1.8kg) whole wheat flour plus 1 cup (225g) for kneading

1/2 cup (150ml) water

1/2 cup (150ml) vegetable oil

3 cups (675g) sponge (see page 33)

2 tablespoons toasted sesame seed (optional)

Have ingredients at room temperature. In a large bowl, beat 4 eggs, salt, honey, flour, water, and oil. Blend thoroughly. Add the sponge. Turn onto a floured board and knead for 10 minutes. Place dough in a bowl, cover, and let rise in a warm place for 3 to 5 hours.

Turn back on floured board and divide dough into 2 pieces. Divide each piece into thirds and roll the 6 pieces into ropes about 12 inches (300mm) long. Braid pieces together into a loaf, pushing the ends together. Place on an oiled baking sheet and slit the top of each section.

Let rise again in a warm place for about 2 hours. Preheat the oven to 350°F (180°C, Gas mark 4). Beat remaining egg and brush tops. Sprinkle with sesame seed. Bake 30 to 40 minutes. Turn oven off and leave loaves in an additional 5 minutes. Loaves should shake free of pans. Cool on racks. Challah can be frozen.

Braids may be curled into a circle. Four braids may be used instead of three. The fourth braid is narrower than the others and placed atop the loaf.

Apricot Raisin Sourdough Bread

When David was a little past the top of the mountain, there was Ziba the servant of Mephibosheth, who met him with a couple of saddled donkeys, and on them two hundred loaves of bread, one hundred clusters of raisins, one hundred summer fruits, and a skin of wine.
2 Samuel 16:1

1 cup (225g) sponge (see page 33)

1 cup (225g) applesauce

2 cups (450g) whole wheat flour plus extra for kneading

1 teaspoon salt

2 tablespoons honey, barley malt, or date syrup

11/2 tablespoons vegetable oil

2 teaspoons cinnamon

1/2 cup (125g) chopped fresh or dried apricots, soaked in apricot nectar to cover

1/2 cup (125g) raisins, soaked in apple juice to cover

Have all ingredients at room temperature. Combine and turn mixture onto floured board for kneading. Knead at least 10 minutes. Form a loaf, slit the top, and brush with water. Allow to sit for at least 2 hours in a warm place. If loaf loses its shape from overproofing, simply reknead and reshape. Brush top of loaf with water to conserve moisture. Brush again while baking. Preheat oven to 375°F (190°C, Gas mark 5) and bake for 1 hour. This bread keeps well and is delightful for sandwiches or cinnamon toast, or spread with Apricot Curd.

Carob Spicery Seed Bread

And they sat down to eat a meal. Then they lifted their eyes and looked, and there was a company of Ishmaelites, coming from Gilead with their camels, bearing spices, balm, and myrrh, on their way to carry them down to Egypt. Genesis 37:25

3 cups (675g) sponge (see page 33)

3 cups (675g) whole wheat flour

1/2 cup (125g) carob flour

2 tablespoons vegetable oil

2 teaspoons cinnamon

4 tablespoons honey or date syrup

1 teaspoon anise seed

1 teaspoon ground black pepper

Pinch of cumin

2 tablespoons toasted sesame seed

1 tablespoon poppy seed

1 cup (300ml) yogurt

Warm water

Combine all ingredients into a dough. Knead the dough at least 10 minutes. Shape into 2 loaves and place them on oiled baking pans. Let rise for 3 hours, reshaping if necessary. Carob must be baked at low temperature to prevent burning. Preheat oven to 300°F (150°C, Gas mark 2). Place a pan of warm water in the oven alongside the baking pans. Bake for 2 hours. Let rest in pans 10 minutes before removing.

Onion Board

This delicious bread was traditionally served at, but was not restricted to, the feast held after circumcision of an infant male, which was required by the covenant bctween God and Abraham (Genesis 17:10).

1 cup (225g) sponge (see page 33)

4 to 5 cups (900g–1kg) whole wheat flour

1 cup (300ml) warm water

1 tablespoon honey

3 tablespoons vegetable oil

2 eggs

4 cups (900g) chopped onions

1 tablespoon vegetable oil

Salt and pepper to taste

1 tablespoon poppy seed (optional)

Combine first 6 ingredients into a smooth dough. Knead the dough on a floured surface. Put dough back in bowl, cover, and place in warm spot for 2 hours to rise, until doubled in size.

Meanwhile, sauté onions in vegetable oil until golden. Remove from heat and add salt, pepper, and poppy seeds.

After dough rises, divide into 4 parts. On a floured surface, roll each of the 4 parts into a flat oblong. Sprinkle with sautéed onion mixture. Puncture boards with a fork in several places. Bake on an oiled cookie sheet in an oven preheated to 350°F (180°C, Gas mark 4) for 35 to 40 minutes. Crust should be golden and onions caramel brown. Serve fresh from oven.

Onion Board.

Sprouted Essene Bread

Moisten your wheat that the angel of water may enter it. . . .
Essene Gospel of Peace

The Essenes were an ascetic community that influenced the early Christian church. They were expert bakers of sprouted breads, a technique that produces a sweet, moist, cakelike bread without honey, eggs, or oil. This recipe was in the manuscripts discovered as the Dead Sea Scrolls.

6 cups (1.4kg) hard durum wheat kernels (available in health food stores)

10 cups (2.8 litres) water

1/2 cup (125g) raisins (optional)

1/2 cup (125g) almonds or walnuts (optional)

Use a large sprouter from a health food store or several large jars and porous covering material for the tops, such as cheesecloth or clean metal screening. Use 4 1-quart (1.2-litre) jars, putting 11/2 cups (350kg) of wheat kernels and 21/2 cups (750ml) of water in each jar. Cover the top with a piece of cloth or screening large enough to overlap the edge by an inch or 2 (3–5cm). Fasten the top tightly around the neck of each jar with a rubber band or string, or if using canning jars, the outer canning band without the center disk. Leave kernels in water overnight and drain through the strainer top in the morning.

After 8 hours, rinse the wheat with water and drain immediately without removing the cloth covering. Continue rinsing and draining the sprouts 2 or 3 times a day for the next 2 to 4 days. The sprouts will vary in length. When the sprouts are about as long as the kernel, they are ready to use. Two cups (450g) of kernels will expand to about 41/2 cups (900g) of sprouts.

Use a food processor with metal blade or meat grinder to grind the sprouts into a smooth, sticky mass. Grind 2 cups (450g) at a time for about 3 minutes. With a food processor the dough will first become very smooth, then ball up and break apart. Watch carefully. Immediately after it forms a ball, take out of the food processor or grinder and add nuts or raisins as desired. Shape into 2 or more rounded loaves. Place on a well-oiled baking sheet. Cover and let rest for an hour.

Bake for 11/2 to 2 hours at 300°F (150°C, Gas mark 2) or 3 to 4 hours at 250°F (120°C, Gas mark 1/2). Some cooks feel that the longer, slower baking temperatures preserve the freshness of the sprouted wheat. Up to an additional 30 minutes of baking time may be needed to brown the crust. This bread keeps well and is better if kept a day or two before serving.

Sprouted Ezekiel Bread

Take for yourself wheat, barley, beans, lentils, millet, and spelt; put them into one vessel, and make bread of them for yourself. . . .
Ezekiel 4:9

Ezekiel bread is one of the most specific recipes of the Scriptures. Bible readers will notice that it is not intended as a delicacy for a joyous occasion. Rather, it was an emergency survival food to be prepared during the dire straits of the Babylonian conquest. This version uses all Ezekiel's ingredients except spelt, an ancient grain coming back on the market but not readily available. The passage suggests that the bread may have been sprouted.

3/4 cup (175g) hard winter wheat kernels or spelt if available

1/8 cup (25g) chick peas

1/4 cup (50g) lentils

1/8 cup (25g) unhulled millet seed

1/8 cup (25g) unhulled barley

Sprout the five grains and beans in separate containers, following directions in Sprouted Essene Bread recipe. Start with the barley, lentils, and millet 4 days before baking, then start the wheat berries and chick peas the next day. When your sprouts are ready, grind together following directions in the Sprouted Essene Bread recipe. Shape the dough into 5 or 6 individual patties. Put on an oiled baking sheet and bake for 2 hours in an oven preheated to 200°F (110°C, Gas mark 1/4). Brush tops with water to retain moisture. Turn and bake for another 11/2 hours at 250°F (130°C, Gas mark 1/2). Serve warm.

Meat

. . . You shall not boil a young goat in its mother's milk.
Exodus 23:19; 34:26; Deuteronomy 14:21

Moreover you shall not eat any blood in any of your dwellings, whether of bird or beast.
Leviticus 7:26

Meat was a favorite food of the early Hebrew pastoralists, and the Bible frequently records its preparation as an homage to God. Throughout the first books of the Bible, appeals to God are sanctified by the ritual preparation of roasted animals. The results are often dramatic. After the great flood, God is moved to mercy for the evil of humanity by the sweet savor of Noah's burnt offerings (Genesis 8:21). The priesthood of Aaron is consecrated by Moses in the presentation of a fragrant barbecue (Leviticus 8:22–36). Thanksgiving was demonstrated and atonement for sins requested by the offering of grilled meat. Religious festivals, such as Passover, Easter, Pentecost, and Sukkoth, called specifically for the roasting of whole animals. Offerings to God were always eaten, though certain parts of the animal were forbidden, such as the fat.

The fatted calf

Hospitality and general rejoicing were also expressed through the roasting of fresh meats for guests, as in Abraham's feast for the angels of God (Genesis 18:2–8) and the preparation of the fatted calf (Luke 15:23). Lamb, goat, and beef were eaten.

The Hebrews were very strict about the handling of livestock, setting high standards for purity, cleanliness, and humane treatment. Animals were thought to have the same God-given flame of life as man. This life was in their blood, which could not be consumed. Animals were inspected for abnormalities by the priests and rejected if deemed unfit. Only animals of certain categories were fit for consumption. These laws were recorded in the Book of Leviticus and are known as kasruth or kosher. They remain the essence of an ancient systematic respect for life that distinguished the Hebrews and later the Christians from their pagan neighbors. The laws are still followed by many Jews.

Dietary laws

Those regulations tightened the bonds of community among the Hebrews and discouraged converts to the religion. The Hebrews could rarely socialize with their neighbors over ordinary meals or at the pagan banquets, which frequently featured the pork, camel, rabbit, and shrimp forbidden them. Most ancient societies had rules and traditions regarding the preparation of meat, but few were as strict and ritualized as the Hebrews'.

Many of the dietary laws, such as the systematic inspection of meat and the prohibition against eating scavenger animals, seem reasonable today. Others, such as the prohibition of camel meat, profoundly limited the living space and life-style of the Hebrews. Forbidden the flesh of camels, they could not easily rove the deserts that surrounded them.

Jesus and food laws

By the time of Jesus, these "ancient" attitudes toward food were changing. Many Jews felt the Temple and later the synagogues were not the place for the processing of meat. Eventually these functions were housed separately and put under the jurisdiction of a professionally trained religious authority called the *shochet*. The requirement that no unnecessary pain be inflicted upon the animal was still of utmost importance.

Jesus renounced the kosher restrictions for His followers in Mark 7:19 by declaring all food clean. And as new converts streamed into the church, the Disciples considered which food laws should be kept by those unversed in the ancient Hebrew creed. But the Jerusalem council continued to uphold certain strictures regarding blood and the handling of animals (Acts 15:20). The ancient belief that blood implied life was enshrined in the Christian sacrament of communion.

Roasting and stewing meat with the local herbs and vegetables were the basic cooking methods of the early Hebrews. As the people of the Holy Land came into contact with the Persians, Greeks, and Romans, and new spices and plants became available, their cuisine became more varied and elaborate. In this section we recreate some meat dishes of antiquity, from biblical times through the Roman foods of early Christian times.

A shepherd leads his flock on hills outside Bethlehem.

Veal With Almond Curd Sauce

The hospitality of Abraham to the angels of God is recorded in Genesis 18:2–8. This meal is the occasion of a gift from the Lord. Abraham and Sarah are to have a son, the child for which Sarah has longed, despite her advanced age. At this early juncture, the Hebrews had not received the law against consuming milk and meat together. Veal in a rich cream sauce is still a traditional feast dish of the Middle East, as it has been for millennia.

1/4 cup (50g) freshly roasted almonds

11/2 teaspoons each cumin seed and coriander seed

1/4 teaspoon salt

2 teaspoons ginger, finely shredded

1 or 2 cloves garlic

2 teaspoons honey

2 pounds (900g) veal scallops

2 tablespoons oil or butter

1 medium onion, sliced

1 tablespoon grated orange or lemon peel

2 cinnamon sticks

1/2 cup (150ml) vermouth or light veal stock

1 cup (300ml) light (single) cream or whole milk yogurt

Grind almonds with cumin, coriander, salt, ginger, garlic, and honey in a blender, food processor, or mortar and pestle to form a paste. (If using a blender, add a few tablespoons of the vermouth or stock to facilitate blending.) In a large, heavy skillet, brown veal scallops in oil or butter. Set aside. Brown onion in the same oil or butter. Add almond spice paste to browned onions and gently fry. Add water to keep from burning. Add grated peel, cinnamon sticks, and stock or wine and simmer for 10 minutes. Return veal to skillet and continue to simmer on low heat, about 15 minutes or until veal is cooked through. Add cream or yogurt and heat thoroughly. Do not allow to boil, as this will give an undesirable curdled texture to the sauce. Keep sauce at a simmer. Serve with hot Whole Wheat Sourdough Bread, Basic Barley, and a salad. Serve Sweet Millet Balls for dessert.

Rebekah's Savory Stew

So Rebekah spoke to Jacob her son, saying, "Indeed I heard your father speak to Esau your brother, saying, 'Bring me game and make savory food for me, that I may eat it and bless you in the presence of the Lord before my death.' Now therefore, my son, obey my voice according to what I command you. Go now to the flock and bring me from there two choice kids of the goats, and I will make savory food from them for your father, such as he loves."
Genesis 27:6–9

Stewing was the popular method of cooking fresh meat, and the Matriarchs knew how to make domestic meat taste as rich as game. Here is a selection of stews using ingredients that were available.

Lamb Stewed With Figs and Wine

3 pounds (1.4kg) boneless lamb, goat, or venison, cubed

3 tablespoons olive oil

2 or 3 cloves garlic

11/2 cups (450ml) red wine

1 cup (300ml) water

2 teaspoons dry mustard

2 teaspoons ground coriander

2 teaspoons ground cumin

1 cup (225g) dried figs, halved (1 cup dried apricots may be substituted)

Salt to taste

Trim the meat of fat. In a stew pot, brown the cubed meat in olive oil. Mash the garlic and add to the browning meat for the last 2 or 3 minutes of cooking. Add the wine, water, mustard, spices, and figs. Bring to a boil. Cover and simmer for 90 minutes. Goat as well as large cubes of lamb will require 2 hours to cook. Salt to taste and serve with Basic Barley or Basic Millet, or bulgur wheat, a watercress salad, and Raisin Cake.

Savory Stew With Lentils and Raisins

The ancient casserole dish was known as an *ilpas*. It was broad and shallow with a tight-fitting lid that had a hole for the escape of steam and the pouring off of extra liquid.

2 pounds (900g) lamb, beef, or veal, cubed

2 tablespoons oil

1 medium onion, sliced

1/2 teaspoon ground ginger

1/4 teaspoon ground cinnamon

1 teaspoon ground cumin

5 cups (1.4 litres) lamb or beef stock (bouillon cubes may be used)

1 cup lentils

1/2 pound (225g) raisins, soaked overnight in 1/2 cup (150ml) wine or water

Salt and pepper to taste

2 tablespoons honey (optional)

1 teaspoon orange flower water (optional)

In a stewing pot with cover, brown meat cubes in oil. Add onion and stir as onion browns. Add spices and stock. Cook for 5 minutes. Add lentils, cover, and cook for 1 hour. Add raisins and continue simmering, covered, for 20 minutes. Add salt and pepper. Add honey if a sweeter taste is desired. Stir orange flower water into the stew just before serving. Serve with Basic Barley; Onion, Olive, and Orange Salad; and Fig Cake.

Lamb Stewed With Figs and Wine.

Lamb Shish Kebabs With Roast Barley and Vegetables

The consumption of lamb was surrounded by spiritual significance for many peoples of the Fertile Crescent. The Hebrews considered lamb a great delicacy. The Egyptians valued the milk and wool so highly that taboos developed prohibiting regular consumption of the meat.

2 or 3 pounds (900g–1.4kg) lamb chunks, trimmed and suitable for kebabs

MARINADE

1 cup (300ml) red wine

1/2 cup (150ml) olive oil

1 clove garlic

3 or 4 juniper berries

2 bay leaves

1/2 cup (150ml) apricot nectar

Pinch of cinnamon

Salt to taste

ROAST BARLEY

Prepare 2 cups (450g) barley by toasting on a cookie sheet or flat pan in the oven at 350°F (180°C, Gas mark 4) until lightly browned. Place barley in saucepan with 2 1/2 cups (750ml) water and 1 tablespoon olive oil. Bring to a boil, then turn down heat, cover, and simmer until barley is tender, about 40 minutes. To make barley fluffy, place a dish towel or paper towel between pan and lid after cooking. Let sit 5 minutes.

HOLY LAND VEGETABLES FOR SHISH KEBABS

Parboiled pearl onions

Chunks of white turnip, parboiled or raw

Artichoke hearts

Broccoli flowerets

Parboiled lotus root, in chunks, or water chestnuts

Radishes

Chunks of parboiled parsnips

TO PREPARE SHISH KEBABS

Marinate lamb chunks for at least 1 hour. Drain, reserving marinade. Place vegetables in marinade for a few minutes, then drain, reserving marinade again. On top of stove, bring marinade to a boil, reduce heat, and simmer. Thread lamb chunks and vegetables on skewers. Grill over a charcoal fire, or broil at 375°F (190°C, Gas mark 5), about 10 to 15 minutes, basting with marinade.

On serving platter, place roast barley and top with kebabs. Pour marinade over all. Salt to taste. Serve with Rose Apple Salad, Fava Bean or Lentil Salad, and for dessert Carob Honey Sponge Cake.

Pomegranate Walnut Lamb

(See Pomegranate Walnut Duck, page 52.)

Rack of Lamb With Must Sauce

A rack of lamb is as impressive a centerpiece for a feast today as it was in the time of King Solomon. This roast is garnished with must, mustard seeds mashed into grape jelly, an ancient condiment.

2 racks of lamb (about 2 pounds [1kg] each)

1/2 cup (150ml) olive oil

Salt to taste

Racks of lamb should be purchased from a butcher who can crack and french (i.e., scrape the bones clean from the end of the chop to the eye of the meat) the bones. The bones will need to be covered with parchment or foil during cooking. Preheat oven to 400°F (200°C, Gas mark 6). Brush racks with olive oil. Place in a roasting pan, meaty side up, and roast approximately 25 minutes. Brush with must sauce and roast an additional 10 minutes. If you are using a meat ther-

mometer, it should read 145°F (62°C) for rare. Salt to taste. Serve with Saffron Pilaf and Sumerian Watercress, Figs in Red Wine and Cream, and Pistachio Almond Cookies.

MUST SAUCE

1/3 cup (150g) whole-grain mustard

2/3 cup (300g) grape honey, jelly, or jam

Fresh grapes (optional)

In a saucepan combine mustard and grape honey or jelly, adjusting for taste. Add fresh grapes and heat, stirring frequently until warmed through.

Leg of Lamb With Cumin, Mustard, and Pulse (Beans)

Cumin and mustard, two of the most popular Holy Land spices, combine deliciously to flavor the lamb and beans.

1 cup (225g) pea beans (dried peas)

1/2 cup (125g) chick peas

3 cups (900ml) water

1/2 cup (125g) lentils

1 leg of lamb, trimmed of fat

2 teaspoons ground cumin

2 teaspoons dry mustard or 3 tablespoons prepared

1 teaspoon salt

4 cloves garlic, minced (finely chopped)

1/4 cup (70ml) olive oil

1/4 cup (70ml) wine or grape juice

2 tablespoons whole wheat flour

Soak beans and chick peas overnight. Boil in same water for 1 1/2 hours, adding the lentils after the first hour. While beans are cooking, combine cumin, mustard, salt, garlic, oil, wine or juice, and flour into paste. Rub the paste on the lamb and let sit for at least 1 hour. Preheat oven to 350°F (180°C, Gas mark 4). Place lamb in a roasting pan on a rack and roast for 1 hour. Turn off oven. Add the partially cooked beans to the roasting pan, stirring the juices into the beans. Let rest in the warmed oven for half an hour. Turn on heat to 350°F (180°C, Gas mark 4) and cook 30 minutes more for a 5-pound (2.3kg) leg. Add 15 minutes cooking time for each pound above 5. Serve with Sumerian Watercress, Baked Celery and Fennel, and Pistachio Almond Cookies.

Place into an oven preheated to 450°F (230°C, Gas mark 8). Immediately turn the temperature down to 325°F (170°C, Gas mark 3) and roast 17 to 30 minutes per pound—17 minutes for rare, 30 for well-done. (A meat thermometer may be used; 145°F [62°C] indicates rare.) Forty minutes before the roast is finished, remove from oven

and fill center with cooked barley or bulgur. Glaze roast with pomegranate raisin sauce 10 minutes before cooking is finished and serve additional warm sauce at table. Serve with a Baked Celery and Fennel, Homemade Olives, Fresh Fig and Grape Salad, and Honey Wine Cake.

Crown Roast of Lamb With Pomegranate Raisin Sauce

. . . I have roasted meat and eaten it.
Isaiah 44:19

1 6- to 8-pound (3–4kg) crown roast of lamb (have butcher french the bones, i.e., scrape the bones clean from the end of the chop to the eye of the meat)

4 cloves garlic, mashed

1/2 cup (150ml) fresh pomegranate juice (substitute tart grape juice or apple cider if necessary)

3 cups (675g) Basic Barley or Cracked Wheat Pilaf (see pages 21 and 24)

POMEGRANATE RAISIN SAUCE

2 tablespoons almond oil

2 tablespoons whole wheat pastry flour

11/2 cups (450ml) pomegranate juice (substitute grape juice or apple cider if necessary)

1/2 cup (225g) seedless raisins

1 teaspoon grated orange rind

1 tablespoon brandy

1 teaspoon prepared mustard

Salt to taste

To prepare sauce: Combine oil and flour in a saucepan into a smooth paste. Add fruit juice and raisins. Bring to a boil, stirring constantly. Simmer for 10 minutes. Add remaining ingredients and simmer an additional 20 minutes minimum.

To prepare the crown roast: Rub cleaned surfaces with cut garlic and fresh pomegranate juice if available. Cover the bones with aluminum foil.

Crown Roast of Lamb With Pomegranate Raisin Sauce.

43

Roast Suckling Lamb

And Samuel took a suckling lamb and offered it as a whole burnt offering to the Lord. . . .
1 Samuel 7:9

Serves at least 20

Throughout the Bible there are accounts of feasts inaugurated with preparation of a roast suckling lamb or goat kid. Passover and Easter, the spring holidays, traditionally call for the serving of roasted lamb. In fact, lamb was so intimately associated with Easter that a lamb fashioned of pastry or sugar was often used simply as a centerpiece on the holiday table.

1 whole suckling lamb (about 25 pounds [12kg], or 1 pound [450g] per person for adults)

4 heads garlic (about 30 cloves)

3 tablespoons salt

5 tablespoons ground coriander

5 tablespoons cumin

1 bunch fresh thyme

3 cups (900ml) olive oil

Rotisserie cooking: Have the animal dressed for roasting. With mortar and pestle, crush the garlic, salt, and several sprigs of thyme and spices, and combine with olive oil. Rub all surfaces and cavities with the seasoned oil. Let lamb stand for at least 15 minutes. Push the spit of a large outdoor rotisserie unit through the lamb from breast to hindquarters. Tie the lamb's legs together. Suspend the lamb about 3 feet (1 meter) over a glowing charcoal fire and rotate every 10 to 15 minutes, basting with seasoned oil. The lamb must be watched carefully. Have water close by to keep any flames in check.

Test the lamb after 2 1/2 hours. Determine how your diners prefer their meat, since many people eat lamb quite rare. Depending on size, 3 to 3 1/2 hours will be the maximum cooking time. The outside of the lamb should be crisp and golden. Transfer the lamb to a large serving tray.

Oven cooking: Needs an extra large oven. Place in oven preheated to 450°F (230°C, Gas mark 8). Immediately turn temperature down to 350°F (180°C, Gas mark 4). Oven roasting is best done on a rack with a meat thermometer. Internal temperature should be 160°F to 165°F (71°C to 73°C) for rare, 175°F to 180°F (79°C to 82°C) for well-done. Serve the lamb with a selection of typical Holy Land relishes: grated radish, Must Sauce, brown cumin seeds, black cumin seeds, coriander leaves and toasted sesame seed, mint vinegar, and coarse salt.

The Fatted Calf (Goat or Lamb)

And bring the fatted calf here and kill it and let us eat and be merry.
Luke 15:23

Serves 20 to 30

The return of the prodigal son in the Gospel according to Luke was marked with the roasting of a whole young goat. Sheep and goats were herded together in Bible times and called small cattle. Young goat, or chevon, is today becoming more available in commercial markets. The male of the species must be procured quite young, under 4 months, to ensure tenderness. The preparation of goat is similar to that of lamb, and there are many ways to cook a whole animal without a sophisticated rotisserie. For instance, one can improvise barbecue methods similar to those used centuries ago:

1. Dig a pit slightly wider and longer than the animal (10 to 12 inches [30cm] deep for a small animal, 18 to 24 [45 to 60cm] for a larger one). An auxiliary pit, connected by a trench to the main pit, is useful for starting and maintaining coals, which can be easily moved into the main pit as more are needed.

2. Green branches can be laid across the fire pit to support the animal if substantial cutlery and muscle power is available to turn the roast (which will weigh 20 to 40 pounds [9–18kg]).

3. The best method is to spit the animal. (By the time of Jesus, homes of any means would have possessed iron stakes particularly designed for this purpose. A long iron spit would complete the equipment.) Two forked tree branches of relatively equal height, even whole young forked trees, can be used. Each branch must be inserted at least a foot into the ground for stability.

4. The spit itself is made more efficient if three holes are drilled into it at the approximate places where the hindquarters, middle, and shoulders of the animal will be. Perpendicular skewers can then be inserted through the holes and into the animal to hold it in place. A handle at the end of the spit is also very helpful.

5. The animal is spitted from the mouth to just below the tail. Wiring can be used to secure the animal.

6. Turn the spit regularly, steadily if possible. Brush the animal with olive oil as it cooks. Rosemary branches tied together make a good sop to brush olive oil on the lamb or goat. Season the olive oil with crushed garlic, onion, or shallots, and coriander, parsley, dill, oregano, celery seed, fennel seed, capers, crushed myrtle berries, cumin, and mint as desired.

7. A nice crust should form on the outside of the animal as a result of regular turning and oiling. For a superior crust, mix several tablespoons of honey with the final glazing of olive oil. The heated honey will caramelize, making a luscious brown crust. Date syrup can also be used.

8. Test for doneness by attempting to crack the thigh bone. If the bone moves easily, cooking is complete. Cooking time will be between 3 and 4 hours.

9. The roasting of a fatted calf is not a hurried affair. The fire should be started an hour or more before the cooking begins. Divide tasks so that people can cooperate and take part. Have water handy to sprinkle on flame flare-ups. Serve with Must; Lentil Salad; Onion, Olive, and Orange Salad; and Honey Cakes.

Roast Suckling Lamb.

Saddle of Venison With Hot Apricot Sauce

King Solomon kept herds of deer, roebucks, and gazelle as domestic cattle. Hunting was not a routine manner of providing meat for the Hebrew table, as the animal had to be captured alive and humanely slaughtered according to the laws of Leviticus. First Kings 4:23 specifies that venison was prepared daily for the royal table.

1 cup (225g) beef suet or poultry fat (chicken, duck, or goose) or 1 cup (300ml) olive oil

10 to 15 cloves garlic, slivered

1 6- to 7-pound (3–3.5kg) saddle of young venison

Fresh or dried thyme, marjoram, and oregano

Preheat oven to 550°F (250°C, Gas mark 9). Melt fat in a saucepan, add garlic slivers, and stir to blend, browning slightly if a less pronounced garlic flavor is preferred. Make slits in the venison and insert the saturated garlic pieces. Rub entire roast with the remaining fat or oil. Sprinkle with herbs. Place in oven. Cook 10 minutes, then turn down heat to 350°F (180°C, Gas mark 4) and cook 20 minutes per pound, basting frequently with fat and pan juices. Use the apricot sauce for the last basting, to glaze the meat. Turn up the heat for a time to achieve a crisp glaze. Serve additional sauce on the side.

Older venison needs to be marinated before cooking. Use equal parts olive oil and wine or tart grape juice with additional herbs. Venison is quite lean, so some kind of additional fat will be needed if the garlic in oil is not used. Strips of beef fat, or bacon or pork fat, can be inserted in place of garlic.

Saddle of Venison With Hot Apricot Sauce.

HOT APRICOT SAUCE

11/2 cups (450ml) sherry or sweet wine

1/4 teaspoon cumin

1/4 teaspoon coriander

1 teaspoon dry mustard

1/2 cup (125g) raisins

1/2 cup (125g) slivered almonds

1/2 cup (125g) apricot preserves (unsweetened if possible)

1/4 cup (50g) apricot nectar

1 tablespoon freshly grated citrus rind

2 to 3 tablespoons vinegar (to taste)

1 tablespoon honey (optional)

Salt to taste

Heat sherry or wine and add cumin, coriander, mustard, raisins, and almonds. Simmer 10 minutes, then add all other ingredients except salt. Balance the sweet and sour aspects of the sauce with additional vinegar or honey to your taste. Salt to taste.

Serve the venison with a pickled fish appetizer, Basic Millet, Pan-Roasted Bible Vegetables, Whole Baked Onions, fresh fruit, and Honey Wine Cake.

Roman Beef Sauté With Onions and Ginger

An ancient pot that could be used for sautéing was the *kedera*. It had a rounded bottom like a wok and two handles. The name means "black" in Hebrew, as the bottom was blackened from constant use.

1/2 cup (125g) thinly sliced onion rings

1 tablespoon minced (chopped) garlic

1 tablespoon vegetable oil

2 pounds (900g) round steak, well trimmed and cut into bite-size cubes

1 cup (900g) mushrooms, sliced

2 tablespoons ginger, minced (grated)

11/2 tablespoons Fish Sauce (see page 66)

1/2 tablespoon honey

11/2 tablespoons red wine vinegar

1/2 cup (125g) chopped scallions (spring onions)

2 tablespoons coriander leaves, chopped

Heat oil in a skillet and sauté onion rings until golden. Add garlic and continue to sauté briefly. Add beef cubes and mushrooms. Continue to sauté, stirring. Add ginger. In a small cup, mix Fish Sauce, honey, and vinegar. Add to skillet, stir, and cover. Simmer 4 to 5 minutes, adding a bit of water if necessary. Add scallions and coriander at the last moment. Stir. Serve with Basic Barley, Millet, or Bulgur and Sourdough Fig Roll.

Coriander Beef Roast With Roman Coriander Dipping Sauce

In Exodus 16:31, the taste of manna was likened to that of coriander seed, a plant indigenous to the Holy Land. The leaves, stalks, seeds, and roots of the coriander plant are edible. Coriander is also called cilantro or Chinese parsley.

3 cloves garlic, mashed

3 tablespoons prepared mustard

2 tablespoons ground coriander seed

2 tablespoons fresh coriander root, chopped (optional)

1 3- to 4-pound (1.5–2kg) beef roast

5 stalks celery (optional)

Mash the garlic, mustard, and coriander seed and root into a paste in a mortar or blender. Rub the paste over the meat and let it sit at room temperature for an hour. Roast should be room temperature for cooking. Place on a roasting rack or improvise by laying 5 stalks of celery across the bottom of a roasting pan. Place the meat fat side up on the celery. Preheat oven to 400°F (200°C, Gas mark 6) and roast meat for 10 minutes. Reduce heat to 350°F (180°C, Gas mark 4) and cook 15 minutes per pound for rare, 17 for medium, and 20 for well-done. Let meat rest for 10 minutes before slicing. Serve with Roman Coriander Dipping Sauce, barley pilaf, and a compote of stewed fruits such as figs, dates, pears, and raisins. Honey-Fried Walnuts or Cinnamon Cheese is a nice dessert.

ROMAN CORIANDER DIPPING SAUCE

3 tablespoons Fish Sauce (see page 66)

2 tablespoons water

2 teaspoons vinegar

6 tablespoons fresh coriander leaves, chopped

2 scallions (spring onions), chopped

Combine all ingredients. Let sit at least 10 minutes. This dipping sauce is excellent with all roasted or grilled meats and poultry, hot or cold.

Poultry

. . . also fowl were prepared for me. . . .
Nehemiah 5:18

Poultry was a common food of the Holy Land. Jesus uses the abundance of small birds in the marketplace as a metaphor for God's watch over all creatures (Luke 12:6; Matthew 10:29), and the laws of Leviticus indicate that the offering of pigeons and doves was within the reach of all worshipers (Leviticus 1:14; 5:11). Many wild birds were eaten. The Patriarchs dined frequently on partridge, pigeon, guinea hen, goose, duck, quail, and sparrow. There are numerous biblical references to the hunting and trapping of fowl for the table (Job 18:8–10; Amos 3:5; Psalm 91:3; 124:7).

Water birds such as the duck were particularly abundant in the Nile Valley, where the Hebrews lived for four hundred years. A typical Egyptian banquet might feature several types of both wild and domesticated ducks and geese. These birds appeared less frequently in the drier climate of Israel, and were typically reserved for holidays there. Stuffed goose is the traditional centerpiece of the Chanukah feast. Later, the stuffed goose became a tradition of the Saint Martin's Day feast.

Flocks of quail

The story of the flocks of quail provided for the Hebrews wandering in the Sinai (Numbers 11:32; Exodus 16:13) conforms to the still observable migratory patterns of this bird. During the European winter, flocks of quail migrate south over the Holy Land. Shifts in the wind often cause large numbers to fall onto the Sinai plains.

The introduction of chicken to the Holy Land cannot be accurately dated, though the bird is known to have originated among the Indus Valley civilizations. A painting from the tomb of Tutankhamen of about 1350 B.C. shows a typical barnyard rooster. This particular chicken was most likely an exotic, prized pet of the Pharaoh, not the common farm fixture it became.

Other sources claim the chicken arrived through the Persian trade routes a few centuries before the Christian era, a claim substantiated in the Bible. Although the Hebrew Scriptures do not mention the chicken, there are references to it in three of the Gospels (Matthew 26:34; Luke 13:34; 22:34; and Mark 14:30). By the eighth century B.C., the chicken was known to the Assyrians as "the bird that lays an egg every day." And the Romans were so familiar with the domestic chicken that dinners generally began with an egg course, a custom recalled in the Passover meal.

The cookbook of the Roman Apicius contains over 25 recipes for poultry. Grilling, stewing, and roasting with herbs and vegetables seem to have been popular cooking methods for poultry, as they are today. Creamed chicken, chicken with wine sauces, and cold chicken salads were common Roman dishes. A banquet might have featured baked flamingo, ostrich, crane, and peacock. A small bird called the figpecker was a special delicacy, as its flesh was sweet from a diet of fruit.

An Arab woman sells chickens at the traditional market in Beersheba, southern Israel.

Chicken With Sage in a Clay Pot.

Chicken With Sage in a Clay Pot

Serves 4

Sage grows wild in most Mediterranean countries and has since early times been used as a flavoring in cooking, fresh or dried, and as a salad green when fresh. The biblical type, *Salvia judaica*, is not available here, but our common sage can be substituted and has much the same taste.

1 4-pound (2kg) chicken

2 tablespoons olive oil

1/2 cup (25g) parsley, minced (finely chopped)

1/2 cup (25g) chopped celery

1 tablespoon dried sage leaves, crumbled, or 3 tablespoons fresh

3 carrots, sliced

3 small turnips, sliced

12 tiny white (pearl) onions, peeled

1/2 cup (150ml) dry white wine (optional)

Salt and pepper to taste

Soak a clay pot in cool water for 25 minutes. Meanwhile, wash the chicken, pat dry, and rub with olive oil. Rub chicken cavity and outside skin with parsley and sage. Add salt and pepper. Place chicken in the pot, adding vegetables around inside and on top of chicken. Add wine if using. Cover with presoaked top of clay pot and place in a cold oven. Turn heat to 450°F (230°C, Gas mark 8) and bake for 65 minutes. Remove the top to crisp the chicken for the final 10 minutes of cooking. During browning, remove the vegetables that are on top of the chicken. Replace after browning. Serve chicken from the pot, which will have rich juices on the bottom. Basic Barley or Millet complements the chicken and sauce.

Roast Chicken Stuffed With Fried Onions and Nuts

This tasty chicken recipe was translated from ancient Mesopotamian clay tablets. As with most ancient recipes, exact quantities of ingredients were not given, so we experimented to develop exact amounts.

1 teaspoon whole coriander seed

1 teaspoon fennel seed

1 teaspoon whole brown cumin seed

1/2 teaspoon whole celery seed

1 juniper berry

1 tablespoon dried pomegranate seed (optional)

Dash of cinnamon

8 large onions, finely chopped

3 tablespoons olive oil

5 tablespoons almonds or pine nuts

1 large roasting chicken

2 regular-size disks whole wheat pita bread

3 cups (675g) Basic Barley (see p. 21) or Basic Bulgur (see p. 22)

Salt to taste

In a mortar or clean coffee grinder, grind spices into a powder. Already ground spices may be substituted, but adjust quantities slightly upward. Reserve. Preheat oven to 350°F (180°C, Gas mark 4).

In a skillet, sauté onions in 2 tablespoons olive oil until lightly golden. Drain onions on paper towels to remove as much oil as possible. Sauté nuts in remaining tablespoon oil. Drain as with onions. Combine ground spices, nuts, and onions, and stuff chicken with mixture, reserving 2/3 cup (150g) for topping. Bake chicken in tightly covered dish or foil for 11/2 hours. Uncover and cook for an additional half hour, basting frequently with pan juices. To serve, line a warm serving dish with pita bread, spoon pan juices and warm, cooked grain on bread, and place chicken on top. Top with reserved onion, nut, and spice mixture. Salt to taste. Accompany with bowls of olives and a salad of mixed greens, and serve Fresh Berry Puree for dessert.

Chicken Braised With Spinach and Prunes

This Persian combination is so delicious that it should be easy for you to get the family to eat both spinach and prunes. Queen Esther accomplished just such miracles of persuasion at the feasts she gave for King Ahasueras (Esther 5:4; 7:1).

1 large onion, sliced

1/2 teaspoon cinnamon

1 teaspoon turmeric

2 tablespoons chicken fat, oil, or butter

2 cloves garlic, minced (crushed)

4 pounds (1.8kg) chicken pieces

1 cup (300ml) chicken stock

1/4 cup (70ml) tart grape juice, lemon juice, or vinegar

1/2 cup (150ml) water

2 pounds (900g) fresh spinach or 20 ounces (575g) frozen (do not thaw)

10 pitted prunes

Dash of cumin

2 bunches scallions (spring onions), chopped

1/2 teaspoon grated citron (lemon) peel (optional)

Salt to taste

Walnut pieces

In a Dutch oven, sauté the onion with cinnamon and turmeric in oil, fat, or butter for 3 minutes. Add garlic. Then add chicken pieces and brown. Add all other ingredients (except salt and walnuts), cover, and simmer for 40 minutes or until the chicken is cooked, adding more water if necessary. Salt to taste. Add additional spices if desired. Garnish with walnut pieces. Serve with lentils and rice, or Basic Millet, and a selection of biblical fruits and cheeses.

Baked Mustard Chicken Teimah

The golden-flowered mustard plant yielded abundant seeds and greens for the biblical kitchen. Jesus mentioned the beneficence of the mustard plant in three of the Gospels (Matthew 17:20; Mark 4:32; and Luke 13:19).

4 pounds (1.8kg) chicken pieces

4 tablespoons sharp prepared mustard

1 tablespoon dried dill or thyme or 3 tablespoons fresh

1/2 cup (125g) whole wheat bread crumbs (see below)

Rub chicken pieces with mustard. Combine herb and bread crumbs. Coat chicken pieces with crumb mixture by dredging on a plate or dropping pieces into a bag and shaking. Place chicken on a large, flat baking pan. Bake at 350°F (180°C, Gas mark 4) for an hour. Covering the chicken will result in a "smothered" effect with gravy.

Uncovered, the chicken will have a dry, crispy crust. Serve with Yogurt Soup, Baked Celery and Fennel, Onion Board, and Figs in Red Wine and Cream or Haroseth.

Whole wheat bread crumbs: For every 1/2 cup (125g), toast 4 slices of bread until crisp and dry. Tear in pieces and whirl through blender.

Roman Marinade for Grilled Chicken

Fermented fish sauces were among the most prized condiments of imperial Rome. The legacy of fish sauce is the frequent appearance of anchovies in contemporary Italian cooking.

4 pounds (1.8kg) chicken pieces

MARINADE

1 teaspoon ground black pepper

5 tablespoons olive oil

4 cloves garlic, mashed (crushed)

1 teaspoon celery seed

3 tablespoons Fish Sauce (see page 66)

2 teaspoons honey

1/2 teaspoon dry mustard

1 teaspoon each dried dill, mint, lovage, and rue* if available (if using fresh herbs, triple the quantity)

In a large, shallow pan, combine the marinade ingredients and rub over the chicken pieces. Let sit at least an hour or as long as overnight, refrigerated. Turn pieces occasionally. Bake, broil, or grill chicken. Marinade should be boiled before serving as a sauce. This is also an excellent marinade for chunks of boneless chicken. Serve with other Roman-style foods such as Roman Asparagus or Cruciferous Vegetable Bake.

* See note on p. 12

Opposite: Baked Mustard Chicken Teimah and Roman Marinade for Grilled Chicken.

Duck in Grape Juice

. . . and I took the grapes and pressed them into Pharaoh's cup. . . .
Genesis 40:11

2 5-pound (2.5kg) ducks (domestic or wild), 3 ducks if not using breasts

11/2 cups (350g) whole wheat or barley flour

1 cup (300ml) cooking oil

4 cups (1.2 litres) grape juice

1/2 cup (150ml) red wine or red wine vinegar

Salt and pepper to taste

Cut up the ducks as you would a chicken. (The breasts may be excluded from this dish if saving them is preferred.) Salt the duck and roll in the flour. In a large skillet, fry pieces in oil until golden brown. Pour off the oil and add the grape juice and wine or wine vinegar. Cook over medium heat for another 40 minutes or until duck is tender. Salt and pepper to taste. Serve with Basic Wheat Kernels, Coriander Relish, Endive With Olives and Raisins, and Whole Wheat Sourdough Bread.

Roman Chicken Salad With Fresh Peas

The Romans loved elaborate combinations. Fish, chicken, and veal might appear in a single dish. This salad includes peas, a favorite Roman vegetable to which Apicius devoted an entire chapter of his cookbook.

2 cups (450g) shredded romaine (cos) lettuce

2 cups (450g) cooked chicken meat, skin removed

1 cup (225g) fresh peas, steamed (use canned if necessary)

3 hard-boiled eggs

1/4 cup (50g) small pitted olives

3 to 5 anchovy fillets, chopped

1 tablespoon capers

1 cup (225g) diced celery

4 tablespoons toasted almonds

Combine salad ingredients. Toss with Vinaigrette Dressing before serving.

VINAIGRETTE DRESSING

1 teaspoon honey

1 garlic clove, crushed (optional)

1 tablespoon prepared mustard

1/4 teaspoon celery seed

1 cup (300ml) olive oil

1/2 cup (150ml) vinegar

Salt to taste

Mash honey, garlic, mustard, and celery seed. Add oil slowly, stirring constantly. Add vinegar. Salt to taste. Date Nut Bread or Onion Board will round out a light meal.

Grilled Breast of Duck With Rose Vinegar

Rose vinegar, jams, and sauces were luxury condiments in the ancient world. If you have a rose garden, you can prepare your own rose vinegar. Take fresh unsprayed petals. Place in a bottle and cover with white vinegar. Store several weeks before using. The process can be hastened by heating the vinegar to near boiling before combining with the petals. If you cannot obtain rose vinegar, flavor white vinegar with rose water, 1 teaspoon rose water to 2 tablespoons vinegar. Rose flavoring can overwhelm the uninitiated, so use sparingly and taste as you go along.

3 boneless duck breasts (preferably large, meaty ones; chicken breasts may be substituted)

1/2 cup (125g) duck or chicken fat

2 cups (600ml) rich duck or chicken stock

3 teaspoons to 3 tablespoons rose vinegar

or 1 teaspoon rose water plus 2 tablespoons white vinegar (or to taste)

1/2 cup (125g) fresh parsley, chopped

Candied rose petals (optional)

Salt to taste

Skin the duck breasts. Sauté the skin in a small amount of duck fat until crisp. Chop and save for finished dish. Pound duck breasts into flat 1/4-inch (7mm) slabs. Brush with duck fat on both sides. Broil in the oven or over medium-hot charcoal 3 to 5 minutes per side.

Boil 2 cups (600ml) of stock until reduced to approximately 2/3 cup (200ml). Add rose vinegar to taste. Reduce final mixture to about 1/2 cup (150ml). To serve, slather grilled duck breast with rose vinegar sauce and crisp skin pieces. Garnish with parsley and candied rose petals. Salt. Serve with Saffron Pilaf, steamed spinach, crisp radish roses in a salad, and Fennel Seed Cake.

Pomegranate Walnut Duck or Chicken

Queen Esther gave two feasts to win the favor of the Persian King Ahasuerus. Among the delicacies would have been Pomegranate Walnut Sauce on duck, chicken, or lamb. This sauce, the pride of the Persian kitchen, is a classic, and every Persian cook perfects an irresistible version. Experiment with the suggested spices and adjust the tartness and sweetness to your liking with fresh lemon and honey.

2 onions, chopped

4 tablespoons butter or oil

2 ducks or chickens cut in eighths

1 cup chicken stock (canned, if necessary)

1 cup pomegranate juice, fresh (see below), canned, or reconstituted syrup mixed with fresh lemon juice

21/2 cups (575g) ground walnuts

1/2 teaspoon each cinnamon, clove, honey, pepper, cumin

Roman Chicken Salad With Fresh Peas.

Salt to taste

Pomegranate seed

Walnut halves

In a large skillet, sauté the chopped onions in butter or oil until they are golden brown. Remove onions and sauté the duck or chicken pieces. Return the onions to the skillet. Add stock and simmer for 15 minutes. Skim fat from surface. Add pomegranate juice, ground walnuts, and seasonings. Cover and simmer for 20 to 40 min-utes or until poultry is cooked. Season further with salt if desired. Add water if sauce appears to be drying up. Serve on a bed of cooked barley or wheat. Garnish with fresh pomegranate seed and walnuts. The choice of canned, fresh, or reconstituted pomegranate juice will determine the need for honey and lemon. Canned juices will definite-ly need the tartness of fresh lemon.

FRESH POMEGRANATE JUICE
To extract juice from fresh pomegran-ates, first roll them along a hard sur-face to soften. Then cut in half and use an orange squeezer, or squeeze juice out by pressing halves with your hands over a bowl.

Be sure to try this recipe substituting 3 pounds (1.4kg) of boneless lamb chunks for the duck or chicken. For a delightful Persian-style meal, begin with Cardoon Soup, serve the chicken, duck, or lamb with Basic Parched Wheat or Millet and steamed spinach, and try baked apples or Pistachio Snow Sherbet for dessert.

Chicken Phyllo Pie

Serves 12 to 16

As a firstborn male child, Jesus was presented at the Temple in Jerusalem. Mary and Joseph, who made this pilgrimage to present the infant to God (Luke 2:22–24), also provided the offering of young pigeons, customary upon the birth of all children. This traditional pie, rich with nuts, eggs, and poultry, is still perfect for the celebration of a new arrival.

2 1/2 pounds (1kg) boneless chicken or pigeon meat (chicken thighs are close in texture to pigeon meat)

4 cloves garlic, mashed to a paste with salt (optional)

3 cups (900ml) water

1 large onion, finely chopped

1/4 cup (50g) parsley, chopped

1 1/2 cups (350g) butter or (450ml) almond oil

1 teaspoon ground coriander

3/4 teaspoon ground ginger

1/2 teaspoon saffron threads, crushed (optional)

3 cinnamon sticks

2 cups (450g) blanched almonds

4 tablespoons honey

1 1/4 teaspoons ground cinnamon

1/3 cup (150ml) grape juice or lemon juice

10 eggs

16 leaves of phyllo (filo) dough

Salt and pepper to taste

Rub the poultry with the garlic paste if desired and let sit for 10 minutes. Then wipe off the garlic paste. In a large pot, put poultry, water, onion, parsley, 1/2 cup (125g) butter or (150ml) oil, coriander, ginger, saffron, cinnamon sticks, salt, and pepper. Bring to a boil, then simmer for 30 minutes to 1 hour. Remove chicken meat and chop. Discard cinnamon sticks.

Sauté the almonds in a teaspoon of butter or oil and put through grinder. Combine with honey and ground cinnamon.

Over high heat, reduce the liquid in which the chicken was cooked to about 2 cups (600ml). Add grape or lemon juice. Whisk the eggs and add to the simmering liquid, stirring constantly. Allow the eggs to cook to the consistency of yogurt. Transfer to a bowl. The cinnamon-scented nuts, the egg custard, and the spiced chicken meat compose the filling of the pie.

ASSEMBLING THE PIE
Have phyllo leaves ready with additional cup of melted butter or oil nearby. Phyllo leaves should be covered with a damp cloth to retain moisture. Work with a pastry brush or hands, patting the leaves with butter or oil. Phyllo leaves are quite fragile, but tears can be repaired by pinching dough together with buttered fingers. In a 12-inch-round (30cm) ovenproof skillet or baking pan brushed with oil or butter, place 6 phyllo leaves, each oiled. Overlap the sides. Fold 2 additional oiled phyllo leaves in half and place in the center of pan. Sprinkle the almond mixture over the phyllo leaves.

Spread half the egg mixture over the phyllo, followed by the poultry pieces, then the last of the egg mixture. Fold the overlapping phyllo pieces over this. Place the remaining phyllo leaves, all oiled, over the top, tucking them around the sides to cover. Bake in an oven preheated to 425°F (220°C, Gas mark 7) for 20 minutes or until golden. Invert the chicken pie on a cookie sheet, but do not remove original baking pan. Bake for an additional 10 minutes. Remove baking pan so top can toast to a crisp light gold. Serve pie on cookie sheet or reapply baking pan and flip over if necessary for storage. Before slicing, allow pie to cool slightly. Sprinkle with cinnamon and powdered sugar. Cut into diamond wedges and serve immediately. Olives, a mixed green salad, creamed spinach, and broccoli garnished with pine nuts and capers are good accompaniments.

Grilled Marinated Quail

So it was that quails came up at evening and covered the camp. . . .
Exodus 16:13

6 to 10 quail, dressed

6 cloves garlic

6 juniper berries, cracked

4 scallions (spring onions), chopped

1 cup (300ml) dry white wine or apple juice

2 teaspoons cumin

2 teaspoons coriander seed

1/2 cup (150ml) olive oil

5 tablespoons coriander leaves or parsley, finely chopped

In a shallow pan large enough to hold quail, combine all ingredients, except quail, into a marinade. Add the quail, coating all sides with sauce. Marinate quail for an hour, longer if desired. Drain, reserving marinade. Place marinade in a saucepan and bring to a boil. Place on grill to simmer while birds cook.

To grill quail, begin with breast side to the fire. Baste with cooked marinade. Grill for 2 to 3 minutes, turn, and grill another minute or 2. Breast meat should be firm but not dry. Serve marinade as sauce with quail. We recommend this dish as an appetizer. For a main course, double the quantities. Serve with Cucumbers Stuffed With Barley and Raisins, and Wheat Pilaf, Apple Rose Salad, and Pistachio Almond Cookies.

Grilled Cornish Hens With Mint Garlic Marinade

We are substituting readily available Cornish hens (or poussins) for the pigeons, doves, partridges, and other small birds enjoyed by people of the Bible, but use these other small birds if you wish.

Chicken Phyllo Pie.

1/2 cup (150ml) olive oil

7 cloves garlic, crushed

2 tablespoons Fish Sauce (see page 66)

4 tablespoons honey

2 tablespoons vinegar

1 cup (300ml) white wine

1 cup (225g) torn fresh mint leaves or 1/3 cup (150g) dried

6 Cornish game hens (poussins), halved or quartered

Fresh mint sprigs

Combine oil, garlic, Fish Sauce, honey, vinegar, wine, and mint leaves. Pour over cleaned birds and rub on all surfaces. Let stand at least 1 hour or as long as overnight, refrigerated. Prepare a charcoal fire. Drain marinade and reserve. Mount birds on skewers and grill for 45 minutes to an hour, turning every 15 minutes. In a saucepan, bring reserved marinade to a boil and simmer gently for a few minutes. Serve as a sauce. Garnish birds with fresh mint. Goes well with Basic Barley or Wheat Pilaf, Whole Wheat Pita, Three Sprout Salad, and fresh fruit for dessert.

Partridges or Cornish Hens With Nuts

. . . as when one hunts a partridge in the mountains.
1 Samuel 26:20

1 cup (300ml) white wine

1/2 cup (150ml) olive oil plus 3 table-spoons poultry fat or oil

1 teaspoon ground coriander

2 tablespoons honey

5 shallots or green onions

1 bay leaf

1/3 cup (70ml) vinegar

2 teaspoons dried or 2 tablespoons fresh thyme

Salt to taste

6 partridges or Cornish game hens (poussins), quartered

1 onion, sliced

1/2 cup (125g) almonds, walnuts, or pistachios (or a combination)

1/2 cup (150ml) date, apricot, or grape brandy

Combine wine, oil, coriander, honey, shallots, bay leaf, vinegar, thyme, and salt. Marinate the birds for several hours, turning frequently. Remove and dry birds, reserving marinade. Brown onion in fat. Add birds and brown. Reduce heat, cover, and cook gently for about 20 to 30 minutes. Heat marinade in a separate pan. Toast the nuts. When the birds are tender, pour brandy over them. Ignite if the alcohol is to be burned away. Sprinkle the toasted nuts on top. Serve with toasted sourdough bread, Sweet and Sour Beets, a green salad with radishes, and Honeyed Cream.

Chicken Pie

Serves at least 16

4 basic Whole Wheat Pie Crusts (see page 81)

1 Chicken Phyllo Pie recipe (minus the phyllo leaves and minus 1 cup [225g] of butter)

The quantities in the chicken pie recipe above will fill 4 pie shells. A quiche with a top crust would be most like the original recipe but will require 8 times the basic pie crust recipe. Layer the fillings as instructed.

If more of a traditional quiche texture is desired, do not precook the eggs. Prepare the pies with nut-and-chicken filling strewn on the bottom crust. Mix the eggs with the reduced broth and pour over the filled pies. Bake at 350°F (180°C, Gas mark 4) until egg custard is set. Serve with Onion, Olive, and Orange Salad; Yogurt Cheese Balls; and a selection of fresh vegetables.

Salty Sweet Eggs

In the Roman dinner, hors d'oeuvres generally included eggs.

1/4 cup (50g) minced (finely chopped) onions

Oil for deep frying

6 hard-cooked (hard-boiled) eggs

1/4 cup (70ml) Date Syrup (page 86)

4 tablespoons Fish Sauce (see page 66)

Coriander leaves

In a medium-size skillet, sauté the onions in 1 tablespoon oil until golden crisp. Reserve onions and wipe skillet. Heat additional oil in skillet or pan suitable for deep-frying. Halve the hard-boiled eggs lengthwise and fry, yolk down, until the eggs are golden and blistered. Drain eggs yolk side up. Remove all but 2 tablespoons of oil from skillet. Add Date Syrup, stir, and cook over low heat. Add Fish Sauce and let simmer for 5 minutes, stirring frequently. Pour sauce over fried eggs,

sprinkle crisp onions on top, and garnish with coriander leaves. Serve with Barley Stew With Lentils and Chick Peas, Ashurey, or Chick Pea Wheat Soup.

See photograph p. 66.

Goose With Apple and Raisin Stuffing

Goose is the traditional Chanukah dinner. Its rich fat content symbolizes the miracle of the small amount of oil that kept the Eternal Light burning for 8 days until more olive oil could be brought to the reconsecrated Temple after the Maccabees liberated Judaea from the pagan Greeks. This miracle of the oil is celebrated for the 8 days of Chanukah.

1 12- to 14-pound (5–6.5kg) goose

STUFFING

1 cup minced onions (sautéed if desired)

3 cups (225g) diced apple

7 cups (675g) whole wheat bread crumbs or (1.8kg) cooked barley

1 cup (225g) seedless raisins

3 tablespoons honey

3 eggs, beaten

Water

Must Sauce, Sour Plum Coriander Sauce, or Candied Beet Preserve (see pages 42, 76, and 68)

Combine the stuffing ingredients and insert into the goose cavities. Sew up cavities or use skewers to close. Arrange stuffed goose on a rack. Prick the skin with a fork. Roast without basting for 15 minutes at 500°F (250°C, Gas mark 9). Then turn down oven to 350°F (180°C, Gas mark 4) for remainder of cooking time. Total cooking time should be 20 minutes per pound based on weight of bird before stuffing. A little water may be added to the bottom of roasting pan to prevent the fat from burning. Garnish with Must Sauce, Sour Plum Coriander

Sauce, or Candied Beet Preserve. Serve with Sumerian Watercress, Roman Asparagus, Three Sprout Salad, and Honey Almond Paste.

HANDLING POULTRY FATS

Duck and other poultry fats obtained from roasting and boiling can be refrigerated and used for sautéing, baking, and enriching other foods. All poultry fats—duck, goose, and chicken—were highly regarded in ancient cooking, especially by the Hebrews, who were forbidden to use suet, lard, or butter with meat. Creamy poultry fat is an excellent texturizer in baking. In savory meat pies or casseroles, poultry fat adds a richness and depth to the flavor. When combined in equal parts with oil or butter, poultry fat has little effect on the taste of baked goods. Poultry fats are not recommended for those moderating cholesterol intake. Keep it refrigerated.

Fish

Jesus said to them, "Bring some of the fish which you have just caught." Simon Peter went up and dragged the net to land, full of large fish, one hundred and fifty-three; and although there were so many, the net was not broken. Jesus said to them, "Come and eat breakfast. . . ."
John 21:10–12

The fish predated the cross as the first symbol of the early Christian church. The Greek word for fish, *ichthus*, was read as an acrostic for Jesus Christ, Son of God, Savior. Because of this association and the many references to fish in the New Testament, it was a popular food with Christians.

The use of the fish as a symbol by the early Christian church harks back to the ancient Hebrew association of the fish with the coming of the Messiah. Some Hebrews believed the Messiah would actually come to earth as a big fish called the Leviathan. The eating of fish at the Sabbath meal evolved from the "pure suppers" at which fish was generally served as a symbol of hope for the future.

Fishing methods
The Bible mentions four fishing methods still used in the Holy Land.

Habukkuk 1:15 describes the use of the small hand net, casting a dragnet, and angling with a hook. Job 41:7 tells of spearing fish with a harpoon. Amos 4:2, Isaiah 19:8, Luke 5:4–9, and Matthew 13:47–50 and 17:27 also mention these techniques.

Forty species of fish are found in the Holy Land. Twenty-two are particular to Israel and Syria. The Jordan River system, which includes the Sea of Galilee, has 14 species of fish found nowhere else in the world and was one of the richest fishing grounds of the ancient world. Indeed, the fishermen of Galilee controlled a lucrative business.

The Sea of Galilee contains warm currents where large schools of fish congregate. Jesus apparently understood these currents, for He gave expert advice to His disciples on where to drop their nets (John 21:6).

Carp, trout, and mullet were among the fish caught.

The Phoenicians supplied the Israelites with most of their marine fish in exchange for grain, as the Hebrews were not a seafaring people. The marine fish available at the Jerusalem fish gate mentioned in Nehemiah 3:3 and Zephaniah 1:10 would have included cod, sole, anchovies, herrings, gray mullet, red mullet, mackerel, tuna, and sea perch. Fish was preserved by drying and pickling.

Sauces
The Romans were extraordinarily fond of sauces made with fermented fish pickles called *garum*, *liquamen*, and *muria*. All manner of fish and seafood were used in their preparation and there were many grades and variations. The cheapest, *muria*, was made from tuna fish.

These condiments compare to the inexpensive dark brown Asian sauces of anchovy, shrimp, or oyster found today in Oriental markets. In Roman times, these condiments could be extremely expensive, particularly those made from the livers of red mullet, the culinary creation of Apicius, the Roman gourmet.

An ancient mosaic depicting the loaves and fishes multiplied by Jesus, at Tabgha, on the Sea of Galilee.

Fish With Honeycomb

. . . He [Jesus] said to them: "Have you any food here?" So they gave Him a piece of a broiled fish and some honeycomb. And He took it and ate in their presence.
Luke 24:41–43

Honey and fish are a unique and tasty combination, one of the specific meals eaten by Jesus recorded in the Bible. Here are some variations.

Broiled Fish With Honeycomb

Per serving:

1/3 pound (150g) firm-fleshed whitefish fillets or steaks

1 tablespoon olive oil

1 tablespoon honeycomb

Vinegar or lemon juice

Rub fish with olive oil and put into an oiled baking pan. Bake at 350°F (130°C, Gas mark 4) for 15 to 20 minutes or broil on low heat for 5 to 7 minutes on each side. Remove from heat and put a tablespoon of honeycomb on each fish steak or fillet. Turn up broiler to high and put fish directly underneath heat to glaze. Honey should caramelize into a light brown. Serve hot or cold with vinegar or lemon juice. Accompany with Barley Cakes.

Honey-Fried Fish

11/2 cups (350g) whole wheat flour

1/2 teaspoon salt

11/4 cups (450ml) water

1 egg

2 pounds (900g) tuna, halibut, or cod steaks, cut into chunks

Oil for frying

1 tablespoon untoasted sesame, olive, or almond oil

2 tablespoons honey

2 to 3 tablespoons fresh toasted sesame seed

Sift flour and salt into a bowl. Make a well in the center. Combine water and egg, beat lightly, and gradually pour into the well of flour. Stir until smooth. Place 3 chunks of fish in a small bowl; pour batter over them. Set aside. Coat all the pieces in this manner. Heat frying oil in a skillet or wok. Fry fish pieces a few at a time until golden. Place fried fish pieces on paper towel to drain as they are removed from hot oil. After all pieces are fried, remove cooking oil and wipe pan clean. Heat a tablespoon of fresh oil in pan, add honey, and heat mixture thoroughly. Add fish and toss to coat with honey mixture. Remove to a serving plate and sprinkle with sesame seed. Serve with Basic Millet and Rose Apple Salad.

Sardines Grilled in Vine Leaves

Then, as soon as they had come to land, they saw a fire of coals there, and fish laid on it, and bread.
John 21:9

1 cup (300ml) olive oil

2 teaspoons salt

1/2 cup (150ml) vinegar or lemon juice

1 tablespoon dry mustard

1 cup (225g) fresh herbs (choose from dill, mint, thyme, bay leaf, oregano, and basil)

3 to 4 pounds (1-4-1.8kg) fresh sardines or 2 pounds (900g) fish fillets

12 to 40 vine leaves, fresh-blanched or preserved in brine

Hot prepared mustard to serve

Prepare a marinade of olive oil, salt, vinegar, mustard, and 1/2 cup of the fresh herbs. If using fillets, cut into 2-inch (5cm), narrow pieces. Marinate the sardines or fish fillets at least 1 hour, longer if possible. When ready to assemble, rinse the vine leaves and dry. Place 1 sardine or fish fillet on the cor-

ner of a vine leaf and roll up cigar-style, tucking in the ends. Use 2 leaves if 1 is not enough. The packages may be secured with string or unwaxed dental floss if necessary. Grill over a charcoal fire, taking care not to burn the leaves excessively. Ten minutes should be enough time on a hot fire. Alternatively, steam or bake the stuffed vine leaves. To steam, use a vegetable steamer in a large pan with a tight-fitting lid. Steam for 20 minutes. To bake, place in a baking pan, add marinade, cover, and bake at 350°F (180°C, Gas mark 4)for 30 minutes. Serve with mustard as a dip if steamed or grilled, and Three Sprout Salad.

Grilled Saint Peter's Fish

Saint Peter's fish, or mushat, is believed to have been the fish that Jesus predicted would contain a shekel for taxes (Matthew 17:27). Other fish may be substituted.

6 small whole fish (such as mushat, sea bream, or mackerel)

1 to 2 tablespoons salt

1/2 cup (125g) parsley, chopped

2 onions, minced (finely chopped)

1/2 cup (150ml) olive oil

1/4 cup (70ml) vinegar

Start charcoal fire or, alternatively, heat broiler. Slash sides of fish with a few diagonal cuts. Sprinkle cavity and outside of fish with salt. Let fish sit for 30 minutes. Place parsley and onion in fish cavity and close with toothpicks or by sewing. Brush fish with oil and place on an oiled grill. Combine the oil and vinegar and baste the fish. Do not cook too close to the flame, as fish can burn on the outside but still be raw inside. Grill or broil until first side is well browned before turning. Brown second side well. Serve with Vegetable Soup with Whole Grains, Sprouted Essene Bread, and Tabbouleh Salad.

Opposite: Grilled Saint Peter's Fish.

Perch With Tahini

We remember the fish which we ate freely in Egypt. . . .
Numbers 11:5

6 medium-size perch or other firm-fleshed white fish

Salt and pepper to taste

2 tablespoons vinegar

3 tablespoons parsley, chopped

1 tablespoon whole wheat bread crumbs

1/4 cup (70ml) sesame oil (not Oriental)

2 medium onions, sliced

2 cloves garlic, chopped

1/2 cup (125g) tahini (sesame seed paste, see below)

Score the fish on both sides, salt and pepper, and sprinkle with 1 tablespoon vinegar. Oil a baking pan and preheat the oven to 400°F (200°C, Gas mark 6). Mix 2 tablespoons of parsley with the bread crumbs and sprinkle over the inside of the oiled baking pan. In a skillet, gently fry the fish in 3 tablespoons of oil until golden on both sides. Reserve oil in skillet. Place fish in prepared baking pan.

In reserved oil, sauté the onions for 2 minutes. Add the garlic and continue sautéing for 2 minutes or until garlic is golden. Add remaining tablespoon of vinegar and tahini to the onions and mix well. Spoon over the fish. Bake for 15 minutes. Garnish with remaining tablespoon of parsley. Serve with Three Bean Soup, Yogurt With Fresh Herbs and Cucumbers, and Honey Cake.

Tahini. Tahini, sesame paste, is sold in many stores.

Once opened, it can be kept in the refrigerator for several months. If you cannot obtain tahini, or need only a very small amount, it can be made from unhulled sesame seeds. Biblical women ground the seeds in a mortar with a pestle, or between two grinding stones for larger amounts. An electric grinder is much easier.

Preheat the oven to 325°F (170°C, Gas mark 3). Toast the seeds for 5 minutes on a baking sheet, preferably one with low sides. Shake occasionally. They do not need to brown. When the seeds are cool, grind in an electric or other grinder until they form a smooth paste. A cup of sesame seeds will make about 1/2 cup of tahini.

Egg-Fried Fish With Two Cumins

Isaiah 28:27 compares the harvesting of two cumins. "For the black cummin is not threshed with a threshing sledge, nor is a cartwheel rolled over the cummin; but the black cummin is beaten out with a stick, and the cummin with a rod." Black cumin is also called black onion seed and *Nigella sativa.*

2 or 3 eggs, beaten

1/2 teaspoon salt

6 white fish fillets (such as trout, pike, flounder, sole, or bass)

Oil for frying

3 tablespoons black cumin seed

CUMIN SAUCE

1 tablespoon chopped onion

1/2 teaspoon cumin

1 tablespoon honey

1 tablespoon ground coriander

Pinch of rosemary

Splash of vinegar

1 teaspoon olive oil

1 cup (300ml) fish or vegetable stock or water mixed with 2 tablespoons Fish Sauce (see page 66)

To make sauce: Brown onions, vinegar, and spices in olive oil. Add stock, bring to a boil, and reduce liquid by half.

To fry fish: Beat eggs with salt. Coat fish fillets in egg batter. Heat oil. Fry fillets in hot oil. Drain on paper towels. Arrange on platter and pour cumin sauce over fish. Sprinkle black cumin seed on top. Serve with Leeks and Cabbage, Endive With Olives and Raisins, French-fried parsnips, and a radish salad.

Poached Fish With Capers

The caper is the pickled, unopened bud of the *Capparis spinosa* bush. In the Bible, the caper is called "desire" and is the plant referred to in Ecclesiastes 12:5: *and desire fails.*

1 5-pound (2.5kg) whole fish (such as weakfish or bluefish)

1/4 cup (70ml) olive oil

1 cup (300ml) dry white wine

1 cup (300ml) water

1/2 cup (125g) fresh dill or fennel or 3 tablespoons dried

4 scallions (spring onions), minced

1/2 teaspoon salt (more if desired)

1 tablespoon ginger, shredded

1 teaspoon capers

Mayonnaise

Lettuce

Whole wheat pita

Lay the fish in a large pot and cover with the wine, oil, and water. Fish may be cut in half if a large enough pot is not available. Add dill, scallions, salt, and ginger. Cover and bring to a boil. Lower heat and simmer for 30 minutes. Place fish on a serving platter, pour poaching liquid over fish, and sprinkle capers on top. Serve with barley and Sumerian Watercress.

To serve cold, remove fish from liquid and fillet. Discard bones, skin, and head. Place fish pieces in a bowl, add capers, and pour cooking liquid over them. Refrigerate overnight. Serve the fish and capers in the jellied broth on lettuce with mayonnaise on the side. Accompany with Whole Wheat Sourdough Bread and Sweet Millet Balls for dessert.

Opposite: Egg-Fried Fish With Two Cumins.

Tuna With Apples and Raisins

The Men of Tyre were the Phoenicians who sold Mediterranean specialties such as tuna at the Jerusalem fish gate. The arrival of fresh ocean catches on Saturdays was irresistible to some fish-loving Israelites, who were then admonished for making purchases on the Sabbath (Nehemiah 13:16–22).

2 pounds (900g) tuna steaks or 3 cans tuna

1 tablespoon butter

1/2 cup (150ml) sweet red wine

6 pieces whole wheat toast (optional)

Parsley or coriander leaves

SAUCE

1/4 cup (50g) raisins

1/4 cup (50g) grated apple

2 tablespoons sweet red wine

2 tablespoons olive oil

1 tablespoon vinegar

1/4 teaspoon ground coriander

1 teaspoon celery seed

1/2 teaspoon oregano

1 cup (300ml) fish stock or water mixed with 2 tablespoons Fish Sauce (see page 66)

Salt to taste

In a saucepan, combine sauce ingredients and bring to a boil. Lower heat and simmer for 25 minutes.

In a baking pan, dot tuna steaks with butter and sprinkle with wine. Bake for approximately 20 minutes at 400°F (200°C, Gas mark 6) until meat is white and flaky, but not dry. Arrange on platter and serve with the sauce. Garnish with parsley or coriander leaves.

If using canned tuna, drain and rinse. Add to sauce after it has simmered for 25 minutes. Serve on toast. Garnish with parsley or coriander leaves. Serve with Vegetable Soup With Whole Grains, and Yogurt Drinks such Grape and Carob.

Sabbath Fish Balls

Boned fish cakes have been a Sabbath specialty for millennia. This ancient recipe comes from the Ethiopian Jewish community, which reckons its descent to the liaison of King Solomon and the Queen of Sheba (1 Kings 10:1–13).

2 pounds (900g) poached, steamed, or baked whitefish fillets

4 slices whole wheat bread

3 onions, finely chopped

6 tablespoons butter or oil

6 tablespoons whole wheat flour

2 teaspoons salt

1/2 teaspoon pepper

11/2 teaspoons dry mustard

1 cup (300ml) milk or water

4 medium dill pickles (gherkins), minced (finely chopped), or 1/2 cup (150ml) pickle relish

1 tablespoon pickle juice

2 eggs, beaten

1/2 cup (125g) whole wheat bread crumbs or matzoh meal

Vegetable oil for frying

Flake the cooked fish fillets and set aside. In a large bowl, soak the bread slices in 3/4 cup (220ml) milk and mash into a paste or put through the blender until smooth. In a medium skillet, sauté the onion in butter until soft. Blend in flour, salt, pepper, and mustard. Add 1/4 cup (70ml) milk and stir. Remove from heat. Add to bread and milk mash along with pickle (gherkin), pickle juice, and flaked fish. When blended, form the mixture into small balls between palms of hands. Dip in beaten egg and coat with bread crumbs or matzoh meal. Fry in hot oil until golden. Serve fish balls with an herbed yogurt. During Passover, these fish balls are always made with matzoh meal.

Fish balls make an elegant appetizer to any roasted lamb, beef, or chicken meal. For a light luncheon, serve them with Vegetable Soup with Whole Grains and Cold Creamed Beet Yogurt Drink.

Tuna Salad With Fresh Fennel

. . . whatever in the water has fins and scales, whether in the seas or in the rivers—that you may eat.
Leviticus 11:93

7-ounce (200g) cans tuna or 2 pounds (900g) fresh

Large outer lettuce leaves (optional)

1 large fennel bulb, chopped into bite-size pieces

1/2 cup (125g) raisins

2 dill pickles (gherkins), chopped

2 crisp apples, chopped

Romaine (cos) lettuce leaves

Sliced radishes

DRESSING

1/2 cup (150ml) olive oil

1 tablespoon prepared mustard *or* 1/2 tablespoon dry

1 teaspoon honey

Pinch of celery seed

Salt to taste

1/4 cup (70ml) vinegar

Wrap fresh tuna in lettuce leaves or foil (prick small holes throughout if using foil) and steam for 30 minutes in a bamboo or metal vegetable steamer over boiling water. If using canned tuna, rinse and drain. Break fish into small chunks. In a small bowl, combine oil, mustard, honey, celery seed, and salt. Beat in vinegar. Into a salad bowl, place chopped fennel, raisins, pickle (gherkin), apple, and tuna. Pour dressing over salad and toss. Substitute a light dressing if desired. Serve on romaine (cos) lettuce leaves and top with radish slices. Accompany with Chick Pea Wheat Soup or Cream of Barley Soup and Carob Spicery Seed Bread.

Opposite: Tuna Salad With Fresh Fennel.

Fried Fish in Radish Sauce

Radishes are one of the oldest vegetables of the Holy Land. All parts of the plant were consumed. The leaves were cooked as greens, the seeds were pressed for oil, and the roots were eaten cooked or grated raw into vinegar for a pungent dipping sauce.

6 fish fillets (such as flounder, sole, or cod)

1 teaspoon salt

1 cup (225g) whole wheat flour

1 cup (300ml) oil for frying

1/4 cup (70ml) sweet white wine

1 cup (300ml) vegetable stock

11/2 cups (350g) grated radish (mild white or red)

Coriander leaves

Chopped scallions (spring onions)

Parsley

Salt fish and coat with flour. In a large skillet, heat oil and fry fish until browned. Drain fried fish on paper towels. Discard oil from skillet; wipe skillet clean. In the skillet, combine wine and vegetable stock and bring to a boil. Turn down to a simmer. Add radish and stir. Add fried fish and heat briefly, about 3 minutes. Garnish with coriander, scallions, and parsley. Serve with Basic Bulgur, Sprouted Essene Bread, and Cinnamon Cheese.

Pickled Fish

Pickled fish was a favorite of the ancient world. Egyptians, Romans, Greeks, and Hebrews were all fond of this flavorful preservation method. Today, availability of fresh, frozen, and canned fish has limited the need for pickling methods and recipes. Still, pickled fish is an excellent low-calorie appetizer.

2 pounds (900g) pike or other whitefish, filleted

4 small onions, sliced

2 cups (600ml) water

Salt and pepper

2 bay leaves

1 cup (300ml) white vinegar

2 teaspoons mixed pickling spices (or prepare your own using dill seed, mustard seed, coriander seed, black peppercorns, and cloves)

1 citron or lemon, sliced

1 tablespoon honey

Wash fish carefully under cold water. Put fish, 2 onions, 2 cups (600ml) water, salt, and pepper into a saucepan. Bring to a boil, then gently poach fish for 10 to 20 minutes or until tender but not falling apart. Place fish in a jar. Strain broth and mix with the rest of the sliced onions, bay leaves, vinegar, spices, lemon slices, and honey. Bring this mixture to a boil and pour into the jar. Cover and shake to distribute the ingredients. Let marinate in refrigerator a day before serving. Serve with Whole Wheat Sourdough Bread, cheese, and fruit.

Salt Fish Vegetable Soup

Dried, salted fish was a staple of the ancient world. It makes an excellent and convenient stock for soups.

8 cups (2.4 litres) boiling water

1/2 pound (225g) dried, salted fish (such as cod; also known as bacalao)

2 tablespoons olive oil

2 cloves garlic, mashed (crushed)

3 tablespoons dried seasonings (thyme, mustard seed, mint, pepper, cumin, coriander, bay leaf)

1 cup (225g) chopped onions

1 cup (225g) sliced white turnips

1 cup (225g) green peas

1 cup (225g) shredded cabbage

1/2 cup (125g) sliced carrots

1/2 cup (125g) bulgur wheat

Pour 2 cups (600ml) boiling water over dried fish and let sit for 15 minutes or until tender. Discard water and rinse the fish under running water. Break or cut up fish into small pieces, removing bones. Heat olive oil in a soup pot and add the fish and onion. Brown, stirring constantly. Add garlic and seasonings. Stir, heating through. Add the vegetables, turning a few times in the hot oil. Add cracked bulgur wheat and 6 more cups (1.8 litres) boiling water. Cover and simmer until vegetables are crunchy-tender, about 20 minutes. Accompany with Matzoh, Pressed Coriander Cheese, and Raisin, Barley, and Apricot Pudding.

Tabbouleh Codfish Cakes

Fish, meat, and fowl were preserved by drying and salting.

1 pound (450g) dried, salted fish (such as cod; also known as bacalao)

6 cups (1–8 litres) boiling water

2 cups (450g) tabbouleh (small-grained bulgur wheat)

3 tablespoons parsley, minced (chopped)

2 small onions, minced

2 eggs, beaten

2 teaspoons cumin

1/4 cup (70ml) oil

Place fish in a bowl and cover with 2 cups (600ml) boiling water. Put tabbouleh in a separate bowl with 4 cups (1.2 litres) boiling water. Let both sit for an hour.

Remove skin and any stray bones from fish. Cut or shred fish into very small pieces. Drain wheat and squeeze out excess water. Combine fish, bulgur wheat, parsley, onion, eggs, and cumin. Run through food processor to achieve a fine mash if possible. Form mixture into balls or patties and fry in oil until outsides are golden and crusty. Turn carefully. Serve with Hot Garlic Sauce (see page 19). Three Bean Soup, Leeks and Cabbage and Fennel Seed Cake are suggested accompaniments.

Fermented fish sauces are called for in nearly every one of Apicius's

Tabbouleh Codfish
Cakes and Salt
Fish Vegetable
Soup (top).

Roman gourmet recipes, and the classical historian Pliny ridiculed his extravagance with these condiments. Many similar products are available today in Asian groceries. The anchovy sauce used in Thai and Vietnamese cuisines is probably most like the fish sauce used in ancient Roman cooking. Ask for "Nuoc Nam" or simply "fish sauce." When using, reduce or delete other sources of salt; small amounts blend well into any nondairy savory sauce. The Roman word garum is similar to the Greek work for shrimp, suggesting a main ingredient in one of the versions of this condiment. These may have resembled the Oriental shrimp pastes or even the Chinese oyster sauces.

From the basis of fermented fish, the sauces were embellished with herbs, vegetables, wine, fruit sugars, and exotic spices. If this all sounds unbearable to your modern palate, try reading the ingredients on a bottle of Worcestershire sauce. This English specialty is a latter-day descendant of the fine Roman fish sauces and illustrates perfectly how the "fishiness" disappears into a pungent, spicy, but very pleasant flavor.

If Oriental fish sauce is not available, make your own.

Fish Sauce

1 2-ounce (50g) can of anchovies

3/4 cup (220ml) wine or water (or mixture)

Combine the anchovies and wine in a small saucepan. Simmer for 10 minutes. Puree the sauce in a blender or hand mash with mortar. Hand-mashed sauce will require straining. Refrigerate.

Recipes using Fish Sauce include Roman Beef Sauté With Ginger and Onions, Salty Sweet Eggs, Grilled Cornish Hens (Poussins) With Mint Garlic Marinade, Roman Cruciferous Vegetable Bake, and Leeks and Cabbage.

Salty Sweet Eggs (see p.56) with Fish Sauce.

Fruits and Vegetables

And God said, "See I have given you every herb that yields seed which is on the face of all the earth, and every tree whose fruit yields seed; to you it shall be for food."
Genesis 1:29

Fruits and vegetables were the only food God provided in the Garden of Eden, thought to have been in Mesopotamia because of the description of its rivers in Genesis 2:10–14. Religious vegetarians base their practice on this vision of Paradise.

The Bible mentions over one hundred plants by name. Terms such as firstfruits (Exodus 22:19) included all the bounty of the harvest—grains and vegetables as well as the figs, grapes, and pomegranates that made up the bulk of the Holy Land fruit crop.

Primitive varieties

Many of the vegetables eaten in biblical times were primitive varieties of the ones we eat today. The Hebrew Scriptures are relatively unspecific as to the then-common vegetables, and much of our information comes from Egyptian, Mesopotamian, and later Greek and Roman records. Plants with edible stalks are simply called herbs in the Hebrew Scriptures, although this group included celery, asparagus, and beets as well as seasoning agents such as cumin, juniper, and bay. The New Testament mentions six vegetables specifically: mustard, thistles, mint, rue, dill, and sprouted grain.

Fruits figure more prominently in biblical lore than vegetables. There were many species of grapes, figs, and pomegranates. An ancient image of peace and earthly happiness was that of one sitting under one's own vine and fig tree (Isaiah 36:16). The time and skill needed to grow quality fruit gave rise to metaphors of patience, nurture, sweetness, accomplishment, and failure. Jesus frequently used images of fig and grape cultivation in His parables.

Round fruits

Apple was a generic name used for various round fruits such as golden apples (apricot), must apples (quince), and Persian apples (citron). Cherries, apricots, peaches, and plums came to the Holy Land via Persia and Mesopotamia. By the time of the Christian era, these fruits were cultivated throughout the Mediterranean area.

The excesses of wine were well known in the biblical world. Indeed, scholars have speculated that the forbidden fruit of Eden was actually a grape. What other fruit, they ask, could so easily have tempted the first couple to disobey God? But if alcohol drove man to sin, the grape was not the lone culprit, for the ancients were proficient at obtaining spirits from figs, dates, and grains. The wine obtained was generally diluted with water and often spiced with cinnamon, honey, and herbs.

The Roman cookbooks of Apicius provide elaborate examples of vegetable stews and spicy cooked-fruit compotes. Salads, combining the green leaves of many wild plants and herbs as well as lettuce, were normally dressed with oil and vinegar. Candied vegetables were very popular, and fruits were sometimes preserved in honey and grape syrup. Further, the arts of preserving in brine and vinegar were well established in the ancient world, and the dill pickle (gherkin) is as old as the Pyramids.

Arab peasants sell fresh vegetables at the traditional market in Bethlehem.

Roman Asparagus

This first-century recipe calls for grinding the fresh asparagus rather than steaming or boiling. The Romans called this type of dish a *patina*.

3 pounds (1.4kg) fresh asparagus

1 cup (300ml) white wine

3 shallots or scallions, chopped

2 tablespoons olive oil

Pinch of celery seed and savory

1/3 cup (150ml) beef, chicken, or vegetable stock

1 tablespoon butter

3 eggs, beaten

Salt and pepper to taste

Fresh coriander leaves

Put fresh asparagus through food grinder or processor to achieve a thick mash. Sprinkle with half of the wine. Sauté shallots in a tablespoon of the olive oil until transparent. Add celery seed and savory and stir briefly. Add asparagus, stock, oil, butter, and wine. Simmer, stirring frequently. As mixture begins to bubble, stir in eggs, keeping heat low. Salt and pepper to taste and moisten with more wine or stock as needed. Garnish with fresh coriander leaves and serve with warm pita bread.

Candied Beet Preserve

Candied vegetables were favorites of the ancient world, and this colorful preserve was traditionally eaten on Rosh Hashanah, the autumnal Jewish New Year, for a sweet new year.

8 cups (1.8kg) peeled and quartered beets

1 teaspoon salt

4 cups (900g) honey

5 teaspoons ground ginger

1/2 cup (150ml) water

2 lemons, thinly sliced

2 cups (450g) walnuts or almonds, coarsely chopped

In a large pot, cook beets with salt in water to cover until almost tender. Drain, cool, and cut beets into julienne strips or cubes. In a large saucepan, combine honey, ginger, and 1/2 cup (150ml) water. Bring to a boil and add beets and lemon. Lower heat and simmer about 1 hour, or until beets begin to have a transparent look and mixture is extremely thick. Add nuts and cook for another 5 minutes. Pour into sterilized glass jars. Store in a cool dark place. Alternatively, store in refrigerator or freezer if sterilized containers are not used. Makes approximately 7 8-ounce (225g) containers. Serve with turkey, chicken, or Roman Ham.

Roman Cruciferous Vegetable Bake

The cabbage family are called cruciferous vegetables because their flower patterns form the shape of a cross. They were popular vegetables of imperial Rome.

1 small onion, chopped

1 bay leaf, crumbled

2 tablespoons olive oil

1 or 2 cloves garlic

1/2 pound (225g) red cabbage

1/2 pound (225g) white cabbage

1 pound (450g) kale

1 head broccoli

1 quince or tart apple

1/4 cup (50g) parsley, chopped

11/2 cups (450ml) dry white wine or apple juice

1 tablespoon honey (less if using apple juice)

1 tablespoon Fish Sauce (see page 66)

Salt to taste

In a large skillet, sauté onion and crumbled bay leaf in olive oil until onion is transparent. Add garlic at the last minute to brown. Add the cabbages and kale, broken up into bite-size pieces. Stir for 5 minutes. Add all other ingredients. Place mixture in an ovenproof casserole. Bake at 350°F (180°C, Gas mark 4) for 1 hour. Shorten or lengthen the cooking time, depending on how vegetables are preferred. Let stand for 10 minutes before serving.

Artichoke Hearts With Spinach and Cream Cheese

12 ounces (350g) cream cheese at room temperature

1/4 cup (70ml) milk

3 shallots or scallions, chopped

1 tablespoon butter

12 ounces (350g) cooked spinach (frozen may be used), well drained and chopped

12 ounces (350g) cooked artichoke hearts or cardoon pieces

1/8 teaspoon dried thyme or 1/4 teaspoon fresh thyme

Salt and pepper to taste

Mash cream cheese and milk together in the bottom of a baking dish. Reserve. In a small skillet, sauté shallots or scallions in butter until golden. In the baking dish, place sautéed onions, spinach, artichoke pieces, thyme, salt, and pepper, and toss with the cream cheese mixture. Cover and bake 30 minutes at 350°F (180°C, Gas mark 4) until hot and bubbly. Serve with whole wheat toast and a fruit salad.

Cardoon Soup

2 pounds (900g) cardoons

1 large onion, chopped

2 tablespoons olive or vegetable oil

4 tablespoons whole wheat flour

8 cups (2.4 litres) chicken or beef stock (bouillon cubes may be used, then omit salt)

2 teaspoons salt

3 tablespoons vinegar

Coriander leaves

Artichoke Hearts With Spinach and Cream Cheese (top) and Roman Cruciferous Vegetable Bake (bottom).

Wash cardoons, and remove large prickly strings and green outer edges. Chop into small pieces. In a large soup pot, sauté the onion in oil. When onion is transparent, add cardoon pieces and stir. Add flour and stir constantly for 3 minutes. Add stock, salt, and vinegar. Cover and simmer for 11/2 hours, or until cardoon pieces are tender. Garnish with coriander leaves.

Baked Celery and Fennel

Celery and its relative, fennel, are believed to have originated in Egypt, where they were called "the door-keepers to heaven." Fennel adds interest to the familiar celery.

4 fennel bulbs, cut into 1/2-inch (15mm) pieces

3 bunches celery, cut into 1/2-inch (15mm) pieces

3 tablespoons butter

4 tablespoons olive oil

Salt to taste

Sprinkling of caraway seed (optional)

Sauté fennel and celery in the butter and olive oil. Transfer to a baking pan, cover, and cook for 30 to 45 minutes in an oven preheated to 350°F (180°C, Gas mark 4). Salt to taste. Sprinkle with caraway seed.

Cucumbers Stuffed With Barley and Raisins

. . . in a garden of cucumbers. . . .
Isaiah 1:8

6 cucumbers

1 onion, chopped

2 tablespoons olive oil

1 cup (225g) cooked barley (see Basic Recipe, page 21)

1 cup (225g) raisins, soaked for 1 hour in

water and drained

1 tablespoon vinegar

2 tablespoons fresh mint or 2 teaspoons dried

1/4 teaspoon cinnamon

Salt and pepper to taste

11/2 cups (450ml) water

7 tablespoons Garlic Mint Relish (optional, see below)

Halve the cucumbers lengthwise and remove seeds, forming pockets. Peel cucumbers only if they are waxed. Set aside. Sauté onion in oil until golden. Add barley, soaked raisins, vinegar, mint, cinnamon, and salt and pepper to taste. Stuff cucumber pockets with barley-raisin mixture and place in a large pot. Add water, cover, and bring to a boil. Simmer for 35 minutes or until cucumbers are tender. Garnish with Garlic Mint Relish if desired.

Quinces, apples, and fennel bulbs may also be stuffed with this mixture and cooked in this manner.

GARLIC MINT RELISH

3 cloves garlic

4 tablespoons fresh mint or 4 teaspoons dried

1 teaspoon salt

2 tablespoons vinegar

Crush garlic, mint, and salt with a mortar and pestle or in a small bowl with the back of a fork. Add vinegar. Sprinkle over stuffed vegetables before serving.

Red Cabbage With Raisins

Apicius, the Roman gourmet, recommended this interesting combination.

1/2 cup (125g) raisins

1/2 cup (150ml) apple or grape juice

1 red cabbage

3 tablespoons vinegar

1 tablespoon honey

Pinch of cinnamon

Salt and pepper to taste

1 tablespoon butter (optional)

Soak the raisins in the fruit juice for at least 2 hours. Cut the cabbage into strips, discarding the tough inner core. Oil a baking pan and place the cabbage in it. Sprinkle with vinegar. Cover and bake at 350°F (180°C, Gas mark 4) for 30 minutes. Add the raisins, fruit juice, honey, and cinnamon. Bake another 15 minutes, more if a softer texture is preferred. Salt and pepper to taste. Alternatively, sauté cabbage briefly in butter in a Dutch oven. Cover and simmer, stirring occasionally for 15 minutes. Add other ingredients and simmer another 20 minutes.

Endive With Olives and Raisins

This unusual vegetable combination includes three of the most abundant foods in the Holy Land. You may substitute other greens, such as escarole (broad-leaved endive), spinach, or red lettuce, for the endive.

4 cloves garlic

1/3 cup (100ml) olive oil

2 pounds (900g) endive, torn into bite-size pieces

1/2 cup (150ml) chicken stock

1/4 cup (50g) raisins

1/4 cup (50g) pitted and chopped oil-cured olives

2 tablespoons capers

Toasted almonds

Salt to taste

In a large skillet, sauté garlic cloves in oil until golden. Discard the cloves. Add the endive and continue to sauté for 5 minutes. Add the chicken stock, raisins, olives, and capers. Simmer for 15 minutes, stirring frequently. Garnish with almonds. Taste before salting, as olives can be quite salty.

Opposite: Endive With Olives and Raisins (top) and Baked Celery and Fennel (bottom).

Biblical Herb Soup or Soup of the Seven Sorrows

Seven bitter herbs go into this soup to symbolize the seven sorrows of Mary, the mother of Jesus. The Feast of the Seven Sorrows, an ancient repast, occurs on the sixth Friday of Lent.

1/4 cup (70ml) olive oil

1/4 cup (50g) whole wheat flour

2 large onions, chopped

2 cloves garlic

1 bunch parsley

1 bunch radish greens

1 cup (225g) sorrel leaves or bunch of spinach

1 large endive

1 bunch mustard greens (use 1/2 bunch if large)

1 bunch turnip greens (use 1/2 bunch if large)

1 bunch coriander

(Beet greens, chards, collard greens [kale], carrot tops, or other available greens may be substituted for those listed)

6 cups (1.8 litres) water

1 teaspoon salt

1 tablespoon vinegar (optional)

In a soup pot, heat oil and slowly add flour, stirring frequently until mixture is a rich brown. Add onions and garlic. Cook over low heat until onion is soft and brown, stirring frequently. Wash and chop or tear the greens. Add to the soup pot and cover with the liquid (which should rise above the vegetables). Add more water if necessary. Salt. Simmer for at least 30 minutes. Taste and add more salt and the vinegar if desired. Sorrel broth, which is sold in supermarkets as schav, can be used instead of part of the water and sorrel.

The exact cooking time varies with individual tastes. These strongly-flavored vegetables are often preferred well stewed. Two hours' cooking time is a general maximum. Croutons are a nice garnish.

This soup makes a fine light meal with bread and cheese. Although it is traditionally vegetarian, the addition of ham bones, meat, chicken, and their stocks does make an excellent hearty soup.

Leeks and Cabbage

Leeks appear to have been the favorite onion of ancient Egypt. Among the medicinal uses suggested in an ancient papyrus scroll is in treatment of human bites. Leeks are still a favorite around the Mediterranean and can be easily grown in home gardens.

5 cups (1.4 litres) water

Salt and pepper to taste

1 cabbage, quartered

4 to 6 leeks

1 tablespoon Fish Sauce (see page 66)

1 teaspoon cumin

1 teaspoon dill

1 teaspoon coriander

1 tablespoon oil

1 tablespoon vinegar

Bring to a boil several cups of salted water. Plunge the quartered cabbage and leeks into the boiling water for 10 minutes. Drain and chop coarsely. Mix remaining ingredients and place all into an oiled baking pan. Bake at 350°F (180°C, Gas mark 4) for 20 minutes. Serve with lamb or grilled chicken. Lettuce can be substituted for cabbage (romaine [cos] is especially good).

Grilled Leeks and Scallions

In the Holy Land, certain areas were renowned for their onions. The city of Ashkelon lent its name to its favorite onion, the scallion.

3 to 6 scallions (spring onions) per person or 2 to 4 leeks per person

Olive oil

Rub the cleaned whole scallions and/or leeks with olive oil and place on the side of a grill over a charcoal fire, away from the direct flame. Some like their onions charred, but for us the perfect grilled onion is tender, cooked through with little dark brown patches on the outside. Leeks will need extra time on the grill. This dish is a simple and delicious complement to any grilled food, especially shish kebabs. Wrap meat and onions up in a fresh pita and serve with a pungent mustard.

Honey-Onion Sandwiches

Across the Fertile Crescent, the standard workingman's lunch appears to have been bread with onions. Here is a delicious version of this ancient combination. It should be made a day ahead of eating.

2 large mild onions, sliced

1 cup (300ml) water

1/4 cup (50g) honey

1 cup (300ml) mayonnaise

1 1/2 teaspoons sharp prepared mustard

Fresh whole wheat bread

1 cup (225g) parsley, chopped

Salt and pepper to taste

Place the onions in a bowl. To make the onions crisp, store them in the refrigerator with a layer of ice on top. When ready to use, drain and pat dry. In a small saucepan, bring the water and honey to a boil and pour over the onions. Mix the mayonnaise and mustard, spread on slices of whole wheat bread, and top with onions. Sprinkle chopped parsley over the onions. Salt and pepper to taste. Serve with soft drinks and a bowl of Pan Roasted Chick Peas and Biblical Cheese and Fruits.

Opposite: Honey-Onion Sandwiches (top) and Biblical Herb Soup or Soup of the Seven Sorrows (bottom).

Whole Baked Onions

. . . we ate freely in Egypt . . . the leeks, the onions, and the garlic.
Numbers 11:5

1 large onion per serving

3 tablespoons rich stock or 1 bouillon cube per onion

Large cabbage leaves (optional)

Peel each onion and remove enough of the top to wedge a bouillon cube in the leaves. Wrap in aluminum foil and bake 1 hour at 350°F (180°C, Gas mark 4). Alternatively, spoon stock onto each onion and wrap tightly. These onions are delicious roasted in the coals.

To bake in cabbage leaves: Prepare onions with bouillon cubes or stock as above. Wrap each in a large cabbage leaf and pack into a baking dish. Cover and bake 1 hour at 350°F (180°C, Gas mark 4). Serve this low-calorie treat instead of a potato.

Pan-Roasted Bible Vegetables

Excavations at Mari, an ancient Mesopotamian site, revealed letters detailing the different mushrooms available in 1800 B.C.

6 stalks of celery

6 large carrots

6 parsnips or yellow squash

2 fennel bulbs

12 large mushrooms

3 tablespoons olive oil

Cumin seed, salt to taste

Wipe mushrooms with a damp cloth. Scrub the dirt off the other vegetables, but do not peel. Chop celery, carrots, parsnips or squash, and fennel bulbs into large chunks. Place all vegetables in a bowl. Pour olive oil over them and mix until all the vegetable surfaces are covered. Place on a flat baking tray. Try to avoid having the vegetables touch each other. Dust lightly with cumin seed and salt to taste. Bake for 30 to 40 minutes at 350°F (180°C, Gas mark 4). A quick turn in the broiler (or under the grill) will produce a nice brown crust if desired. Serve as appetizers, alongside a main dish, or toss with yogurt and a few teaspoons of tahini for a cold salad. Experiment with other vegetables and spice combinations.

Sumerian Watercress

Watercress is thought to have been one of the bitter herbs of Exodus 12:8. Ancient watercress seeds have been found in Egypt, and watercress was among the plants listed in the Babylonian records. Sesame seed was a customary garnish for Mesopotamian foods.

2 bunches fresh watercress

3 tablespoons sesame seed

1/2 cup (150ml) chicken broth

1 tablespoon honey

1 tablespoon vinegar

Dash of cumin

Dash of coriander

Salt to taste

Wash watercress and trim only rough or dirty stems. Prepare 4 to 6 bundles, 1 for each serving. Lay stems together and tie with string. Bring a large pot of water to a boil and plunge in the tied bundles of watercress. Let boil for a scant 2 to 3 minutes. Remove and immediately place under cool running water to refresh. When cool, press out water thoroughly so that bundles will retain their shape when the strings are removed.

Heat sesame seeds in heavy frying pan without oil. Stir constantly to prevent burning. Seeds should begin to jump and pop. Remove from heat and crush seeds with mortar and pestle or nut grinder. Combine with broth, honey, vinegar, cumin, coriander, and salt. Alternatively, place toasted seed in blender with dressing ingredients. Pour dressing over the watercress bundles. Serve in separate bowls or alongside meat, poultry, or fish.

Fresh Fig and Grape Salad

The fig tree puts forth her green figs, and the vines with the tender grapes give a good smell. Rise up, my love, my fair one, and come away!
Song of Solomon 2:13

1 head fresh red-leaf lettuce or other leaf lettuce

15 fresh figs, quartered

1 cup (450g) seedless grapes, halved if desired

MINT CAPER DRESSING

3/4 cup (220ml) olive oil

1/4 cup (70ml) lemon juice or vinegar

1 tablespoon capers

1 tablespoon fresh mint, chopped

Wash and dry lettuce. Arrange lettuce leaves on individual plates; top with figs, then grapes. Mix dressing ingredients and pour over salad or serve alongside.

Onion, Olive, and Orange Salad

The Hebrews seem to have cultivated citrus fruit throughout the Mediterranean, although its exact origin is obscure. One citrus fruit, the *ethrog*, was eventually incorporated into the ritual celebration of Sukkoth, the autumn harvest festival.

4 oranges, peeled, cut up, and seeded

1 red onion, thinly sliced

1 cup (225g) halved black olives (pitted and chopped; oil-cured are best)

Combine oranges, onion, and olives. Chill if desired. This unusual combination does not require a dressing.

Three Sprout Salad

. . . and the seed should sprout and grow. . . .
Mark 4:27

This unusual salad combines the tartness of lentils, the sweetness of sprouted wheat, and the sharpness of sesame with romaine (cos) lettuce, a salad green grown by biblical people. The combination of a bean, a grain, and a seed is especially beneficial since their amino acids complement each other to make a complete protein when eaten together.

SALAD

1/4 cup (50g) dry lentils

1/2 cup (125g) dry wheat berries

2 tablespoons sesame seed

About 12 romaine (cos) lettuce leaves, broken into bite-size pieces

DRESSING

1/2 cup (150ml) olive oil

1/4 cup (70ml) vinegar

1 tablespoon honey

1 clove garlic, mashed (optional)

Start 4 days before you plan to serve the salad by soaking the lentils in water and sprouting according to directions below. The next day, soak the wheat berries and the sesame seeds in separate containers, then follow the directions. When all the sprouts are ready, on the fourth day, combine with the dressing and let marinate for an hour or two, adding the lettuce just before serving. The marinated sprouts can be kept for several days in the refrigerator, if lettuce is stored separately and added at the last moment.

Sprouting Seeds

Sprouting the seeds of beans and grains is a very old method of improving the diet, especially when fresh vegetables were not available. Sprouting is a way of growing seeds quickly through moisture which softens them, starts their growth, and increases the protein and vitamin content.

You can sprout any seeds fit for human consumption, but not garden seeds unless you have gathered your own since commercial garden seeds are often treated with fungicides. As in outdoor gardening, the fresher the seed, the more certain the results. You may be able to sprout seeds from your supermarket (certainly lentils), but other seeds, such as unhulled sesame, can be obtained only at natural food stores.

See sprouting directions in recipe for Essene Bread, page 38, and refer to chart below. Use a separate jar for each type of grain, bean, or small seed. Sprouts can be stored in the refrigerator in covered containers, but rinse daily to keep them alive. They can be stored in the sprouting jar, using canning lids or other tops that fit tightly. They will taste better if eaten in the first few days, but can keep a week under refrigeration.

Sprouts were added to soups, salads, vegetable dishes, bread dough before baking, dips, and pita sandwiches. See recipes for Ezekiel's Bread, Essene Bread, and Three Sprout Salad.

SPROUTING CHART

Grain or Bean	Rinses Per Day	Harvest Sprout Length	Number of Days Required	Yield: Sprouts from 1 Cup (225g) Dry Ingredient
Unhulled barley	2–3	Length of seed	3–4	2 cups (450g)
Chick peas	4	1/2 inch (12mm)	3	3 cups (675g)
Lentils	3–4	1/4–1 inch (7–25mm)	4	6–8 cups (1.4–2.1kg)
Whole millet	2–3	1/4 inch (7mm)	3–4	2 cups (450g)
Unhulled sesame	3–4	Length of seed (Bitter when longer)	3	1 1/2 cups (175g)
Wheat berries (kernels)	2–3	Length of seed (Bitter when longer)	2–4	2 1/2 cups (675g)

Grape Leaves

The Bible mentions grape (vine) leaves only to relate a prohibition against them. Manoah's wife is forbidden to eat them while pregnant with Samson (Judges 13:14), but grape leaves, like fig leaves, were commonly eaten.

40 to 200 fresh grape (vine) leaves

4 quarts (5 litres) water

1/2 cup (225g) regular salt

1/2 cup (225g) pickling salt

Pick grape (vine) leaves early in the summer. Cut off stems and wash, then stack in piles of 20 leaves each, shiny side up. Roll up and tie with a string.

Measure about 2 quarts (2.4 litres) water, add 1/2 cup (125g) salt, and bring to a boil. Drop the grape leaves bundles into the boiling water, a few at a time. Return to a boil and blanch for 3 minutes. Turn the rolls over as they boil so they will blanch evenly. Lift out and drain.

Prepare a brine of 2 cups (600 ml) water to 1/4 cup (125g) pickling salt. Pack the blanched bundles in sterilized jars and pour the brine over them. Remove air bubbles and seal. Wash in fresh water before using.

Alternatively, wrap blanched leaves in freezer bags and store in freezer until ready to use. Besides being excellent for stuffings, grape leaves can be added to soups, stews, and stir-fry dishes.

Rose Apple Salad

. . . Refresh me with apples, for I am lovesick.
Song of Solomon 2:5

5 large tart apples (such as Granny Smith)

Juice of 1 lemon

4 tablespoons honey

2 teaspoons rose water (more if desired)

Candied rose petals

Mint leaves

Crushed ice

Grate unpeeled apples. Add water. Chill. Garnish with rose petals and mint and serve on a bed of fresh snow or crushed ice. Serve with roast lamb, chicken, or grilled fish and as a side dish with Basic Fresh Curd and Yogurt Cheeses and Whole Wheat Sourdough Bread. Rose Apple Salad is an excellent light dessert or snack for children.

Coriander Relish

When the hay is removed, and the tender grass shows itself, and the herbs of the mountains are gathered in.
Proverbs 27:25

1 clove garlic

1 cup (225g) coriander leaves, chopped

1/2 teaspoon cumin powder

1/2 teaspoon salt

1 tablespoon vinegar

8 ounces (225g) yogurt or 4 ounces (125g) ground walnuts mixed with 1/2 cup (150ml) water

Mash garlic, coriander, cumin, salt, and vinegar together in a mortar or whirl through blender. Stir in yogurt or walnuts to make a smooth paste. Serve immediately or refrigerate and serve within 3 hours of preparation. Serve this with grilled chicken, roast lamb, or poached fish, or mixed with mayonnaise as a sandwich spread.

Sour Plum Coriander Sauce

This Persian-style sauce is easy to make in a blender.

2 pounds (900g) fresh plums

2 cups (600ml) water

1/4 teaspoon salt

3 tablespoons coriander leaves, chopped (more if desired)

1 clove garlic

1/4 cup (50g) shelled walnuts

Seed plums and place in a large saucepan with water and salt. Boil for 20 minutes, stirring occasionally and adding more water if necessary. Turn off heat and let cool. Place sauce in blender with coriander leaves, garlic, and walnuts. Blend until creamy. Return to saucepan and heat to boiling. Cool. Store in refrigerator. This sauce is an excellent marinade and basting sauce for grilled chicken and meats.

Homemade Olives

Can a fig tree, my brethren, bear olives . . . ?
James 3:12

2 pounds (900g) fresh olives

6 quarts (7 litres) water

1/3 cup (150g) pickling salt

3 tablespoons olive oil

Fresh olives are generally available in the fall. Pick those without bruises. In each olive cut a few slits with a knife or mash slightly with a flat object. The skin must be broken. Place olives in a deep bowl and cover with cold water. Place a plate on top to weigh olives down and keep them under the water. Change water every day for 4 days.

Prepare a brine of 1 quart (1.2 litres) water with 1/3 cup (150g) pickling salt. Drain olives and put into clean sterilized jars. Cover olives with brine. Add a few drops of olive oil to the top of each brine-filled jar. Cap jars and store for 6 weeks before using. Rinse in cold water before serving. Discard overly soft olives, if any.

SPICED OLIVES
To prepare Spiced Olives, add to the brine:

2 heads garlic, divided into cloves and peeled

10–20 mustard seeds

10–20 whole peppercorns

Desserts

. . . Take some of the best fruits of the land in your vessel and carry down a present. . . .
Genesis 43:11

Fruits, nuts, and baked goods were the desserts of the ancient world. Dried fruit and nuts were winter staples, often crushed together into sweetmeats or stuffed into pastries. The royal kitchens could prepare elaborate desserts—intricately shaped cakes, rich puddings, and even fruit sherbets with carefully transported mountain snow to refresh the palate. Confectioners sold individual sweetmeats in the bazaars and markets, just as today's shoppers are lured by a variety of sweet snacks.

The favorite sweetener of the ancient world was honey. But apiculture came late to the Holy Land, and for a long time only wild honey was available. As the Bible notes, finding a hive of bees with its cache of honey was looked upon as a fortunate event, if not a gift from God. Honey was considered a precious food of exceptional purity and nutritional and medicinal value. The Hebrews were impressed by the fact that honey was produced by creatures as food for themselves. They were forbidden to burn honey on the altar of God (Leviticus 2:11).

Honey in the rock
Honey figures in the stories of several biblical heroes. Moses sang of honey found between rock crevices in the desert, a favorite nesting place for Sinai bees to this day (Deuteronomy 32:13). Samson found a hive of bees nesting in a slain lion and fashioned a riddle for the Philistines from this unusual occurrence (Judges 14:8–14). Jonathan ate honey dripping onto the ground in the forest and was immediately refreshed, though trouble ensued (1 Samuel 14:24–29).

As might be expected, random finds of wild honey could hardly satisfy the sweet tooth of this sugarless world. Dates, grapes, carob, and other fruits were boiled to make thick syrups that are excellent and unusual sweeteners. Sweet wines of raisins, dates, figs, and grapes were also used for flavoring. A variety of sweet substances were collected from insects other than bees. The liquid honeydew secretions of insects such as the cicada condense rapidly in the heat of the Holy Land, leaving a sweet granular residue. Scholars suggest that this edible substance, called manna today, fits the description of the famous manna of Exodus, chapter 16.

The Bible twice mentions sweet cane, in Isaiah 43:24 and Jeremiah 6:20, which may be references to papyrus from which a sweet sap was extracted, as molasses is from sugar cane. By the time of Jesus, small quantities of sugar, called reed honey, were imported from India. Sugar was considered inferior in all aspects to bee honey, though possessed of some medicinal qualities such as aiding in digestion. The Roman cookbooks of Apicius do not include sugar, known also as Indian salt and Asian honey, among their many ingredient lists.

Sweet foods
Ancient people were well-informed consumers of the different flavors and grades of honey. Rare varieties were imported from throughout the known world, with thyme honey especially prized. Guests were honored with sweet foods prepared with fine honeys; the finer the honey, the greater the honor. In addition, honey was used by the early Christian church in baptismal ceremonies.

As beekeeping methods spread, primarily through the Greeks, honey became more widely available. The status of honeyed foods declined, and conspicuous consumption of sweetened foods became associated with overindulgence.

The desserts that follow use honey or fruit sweeteners of grape, date, or carob. Dried fruits and nuts add texture, flavor, and richness.

An Arab trader minds his sweet stall at the Beersheba market.

High-Fiber Fig Cake

The fig is not generally an orchard tree. It grows singly or adjacent to the pomegranate tree in the Holy Land. Simple, nutritious combinations such as this one sustained biblical people through the winter.

1 cup (300ml) boiling water
1 cup (225g) bulgur wheat
1 cup (225g) chopped figs (raisins or dates may be substituted)
1/4 teaspoon salt

In a large bowl pour boiling water over bulgur wheat. Soak wheat for an hour and drain. Add chopped fruit and salt. Put mixture through a food processor or grinder. Form into small balls or patties. If serving hot is desired, shape mixture into a loaf and bake for 30 minutes at 350°F (180°C, Gas mark 4) in an oiled loaf pan. This dish can also be served as a breakfast cereal.

Honey Cakes

The Bible tells of David's triumphant entry into Jerusalem with the ark (2 Samuel 6:13–21). The festivities included dancing and serving honey cakes to all the citizens. This is the legendary origin of the serving of honey cakes for all occasions of great rejoicing, especially weddings.

1/2 cup (150ml) melted butter or almond oil
1 cup (225g) honey
3 eggs
4 cups (900g) whole wheat pastry flour
1 teaspoon cinnamon
1/4 teaspoon salt
1/2 cup (150ml) milk

In a large bowl, cream butter or oil and honey. Add eggs. Sift dry ingredients together and add to creamed mixture alternately with milk. Pour batter into 2 oiled 9-inch (23cm) cake pans. Bake for 35 minutes in oven preheated to 350°F (180°C, Gas mark 4). Top with cream cheese, yogurt cheese, or Honey Sauce.

Fig Pastries

Then Abigail made haste and took . . . two hundred cakes of figs. . . .
1 Samuel 25:18

PASTRY

3/4 cup (175g) unsalted butter
41/2 cups (1.1kg) whole wheat pastry flour
1 large egg
2 cups (450g) honey
31/2 cups (1 litre) milk

FILLING

1 pound (450g) dried figs, chopped
11/2 cups (450ml) water
1/2 cup (450g) honey
1/2 teaspoon cinnamon
1 tablespoon vinegar or lemon juice
1 egg beaten with 1 tablespoon water

To prepare filling, boil the figs in water for 15 minutes in a saucepan. Add honey and cinnamon and continue to boil for 30 minutes more, stirring frequently until mixture has thickened. Add vinegar or lemon juice. Let mixture cool in saucepan.

To prepare pastry, cream butter and flour in a bowl. Beat in the egg. Add the honey and milk. Form the dough into a large ball. Dust the ball with flour and wrap in a damp cloth. Chill for at least an hour, overnight if possible.

Preheat oven to 375°F (190°C, Gas mark 5). Cut dough into 4 pieces. Cover pieces with damp cloth. On a floured board roll out 1 piece and cut into 8 or more squares. Place a tablespoon of filling on each square and brush edges with egg mixture. Fold into a triangle, pinching edges together. Place on an oiled baking sheet. Prick tops with fork and brush with beaten egg. Bake for 20 minutes. Serve with Yogurt With Fresh Herbs and Cucumber for an excellent tea or other light snack.

Fig Cake

And they gave him a piece of a cake of figs. . . .
1 Samuel 30:12

1 cup (225g) butter
1/2 cup (125g) honey
3 cups (675g) fig preserves (apricot preserves may be substituted)
5 egg yolks, beaten
3 cups (675g) whole wheat pastry flour
1 cup (300ml) sour milk, yogurt, or buttermilk
1 cup (225g) walnuts, grated
1 cup (225g) raisins
11/2 tablespoons cinnamon
5 egg whites, stiffly beaten

Cream butter and honey, add figs and egg yolks, and beat until smooth. Add flour and milk alternately. Add nuts, raisins, and cinnamon. Fold in egg whites. Pour into well-oiled 10-inch springform cake pan and bake in oven at 350°F (180°C, Gas mark 4) for 1 hour and 30 minutes. Test to make sure cake is done: A knife inserted in the center should come out clean. Serve with Honey Sauce if desired.

Raisin Cake

Sustain me with cakes of raisins. . . .
Song of Solomon 2:5

4 eggs
1/2 cup (125g) honey
1/2 cup (125g) whole wheat pastry flour
1/2 teaspoon salt
21/2 cups (575g) chopped raisins (dates or figs may be substituted)
1 cup (225g) almonds
Whipped cream

Preheat oven to 350°F (180°C, Gas mark 4). In a large bowl, beat eggs until fluffy. Gradually beat in honey, flour, salt, raisins, and nuts. Pour batter into oiled 9 x 9-inch (23cm) pan. Bake for 30 to 40 minutes. Serve warm with whipped cream.

Fig Pastries.

Honey Wine Cake

This is an especially light and elegant version of the festive honey cake.

5 egg yolks

1/2 cup (125g) honey

1 tablespoon grated orange peel

1 cup (225g) whole wheat pastry flour

1/2 teaspoon (salt

1/2 cup (150ml) sweet white wine

1/2 cup plus 2 tablespoons (160ml) olive oil

7 egg whites

Preheat oven to 375°F (190°C, Gas mark 5). In a small bowl, whisk egg yolks with honey for 5 minutes. Add orange peel.

In a large bowl, sift pastry flour with salt. Gradually stir in egg and honey. Follow with wine and olive oil, stirring constantly as small amounts are needed.

Beat the egg whites until stiff and fold into batter. Line the bottom of an 8-inch (20cm) springform pan with oiled parchment or thick brown paper (cut from a brown paper bag if necessary). Oil the pan and paper well. Pour in batter and bake for 20 minutes. Turn oven off and let cake sit for 10 minutes. It will deflate.

Remove cake from oven. Turn over and detach from spring pan carefully. Serve with wine. Store in refrigerator.

Honey Sauce

11/2 cups (350g) honey

1/8 teaspoon salt

1 egg white

Cook honey and salt to 245°F (118°C) or until it spins a thread and forms a firm ball when dropped into cold water. Beat egg white. Pour syrup in thin stream over beaten egg white. Continue beating until sauce stands in peaks.

Fennel Seed Cake

Also take with you . . . some cakes, and a jar of honey and go to him. . . .
1 Kings 14:3

1 teaspoon fennel seed

2 eggs

1/4 pound (125g) butter

21/2 cups (575g) whole wheat pastry flour

1/2 teaspoon baking soda

Pinch of salt

3/4 cup honey

1 egg, beaten

Toast the fennel seeds for 5 minutes in an oven heated to 400°F (200°C, Gas mark 6). Set aside. In a mixing bowl, combine eggs, butter, flour, soda, salt, and the honey until well blended. Spread in an oiled 12 x 8-inch (30 x 20cm) pan (Pyrex is best for this). Bake for 20 minutes in an oven preheated to 350°F (180°C, Gas mark 4). Remove cake from oven. Immediately brush top with beaten egg and sprinkle on toasted fennel seeds.

Saffron Cake

Spikenard and saffron . . . with all the chief spices.
Song of Solomon 4:14

1/8 teaspoon saffron threads

1 cup (300ml) milk

6 eggs, separated

13/4 cups (400g) whole wheat pastry flour

13/4 cups (400g) blanched almonds, finely ground

1/2 teaspoon baking soda

1 cup (225g) honey

Pinch of salt

Zest of 1 orange, finely chopped

Soak saffron in milk for 1 hour.

In a large bowl, beat egg yolks until they form a ribbon. Combine flour, almonds, and salt in 1 bowl and saffron milk with bicarbonate of soda

in another. Alternately beat in small amounts of flour mixture and milk mixture. Add honey and orange zest. In a separate bowl, whip egg whites with a pinch of salt until stiff peaks form. Mix 1/4 cup (70ml) of egg whites into batter to loosen. Fold in remainder of egg whites until just mixed. Do not overbeat. Pour into 3 lightly oiled 81/2 x 41/2-inch (21 x 11cm) loaf pans. Bake at 350°F (180°C, Gas mark 4) for 45 minutes. Remove from oven and let cool for 30 minutes. Run a knife around edge to loosen, then flip onto a rack to cool completely.

Passover Spice Cake

For seven days no leaven shall be found in your houses, since whoever eats what is leavened, that same person shall be cut off from the congregation of Israel.
Exodus 12:19

The ancient Passover prohibition against leavening led to the development of holiday cakes made with matzoh meal and eggs.

1 cup (225g) honey

12 eggs, separated

1 cup (225) almonds or walnuts, chopped

1/3 cup (150ml) wine

11/2 teaspoons cinnamon

11/2 cups (350g) matzoh cake meal or finely crumbled crackers

Preheat oven to 325°F (170°C, Gas mark 3). In a small saucepan gently warm honey. In a mixing bowl, beat egg yolks, almonds, wine, cinnamon, matzoh cake meal, and warmed honey. In a separate bowl, beat egg whites to stiff peaks. Fold whites into batter slowly. Pour batter into ungreased standard 9- or 10-inch (23 or 26cm) tube pan or two loaf pans. Bake for an hour. Test for doneness: An inserted knife or clean broom straw (or skewer) should come out dry. Up to 10 additional minutes of baking time may be necessary.

Carob-Honey Sponge Cake

Carob flour, the powdered pod of the carob tree, is also called Saint John's bread because of the legend that in the wilderness John the Baptist ate only carob pods and honey.

1 cup (225g) whole wheat pastry flour

1/2 cup (125g) carob flour

2 teaspoons cinnamon

6 eggs, separated

1/3 cup (150g) softened butter

1/2 cup (125g) honey

1/3 cup (150ml) water

2 teaspoons wine or grape juice

Combine flour, carob, and cinnamon, mixing well. Beat egg yolks, add butter and honey, and mix well. Add water and wine or grape juice to egg mixture. Combine the 2 mixtures and stir thoroughly. In a separate bowl, beat the egg whites until they form stiff peaks. Fold egg whites gently into batter. Do not overbeat.

Preheat oven to 300°F (150°C, Gas mark 2). Carob must be cooked at low temperature to prevent burning. Pour batter into oiled 9-inch (23cm) springform pan and bake for 11/4 hours or into 2 loaf pans 7 or 8 inches (18 or 20cm) long and bake for 1 hour and 5 minutes. Test for doneness: When a clean straw or knife (or skewer) inserted into the center comes out dry, the cake is done. As with all honey cakes, this one keeps well.

Whole Wheat Pie Crust

. . . fine flour as a daily grain offering. . . . It shall be made in a pan with oil. When it is well mixed, you shall bring it in. . . .
Leviticus 6:20, 21

7 tablespoons (250g) butter

2 cups (450g) whole wheat pastry flour

1 teaspoon salt

4 tablespoons cold water

Work butter into flour and salt with hands, until mixture forms small pea-sized balls. Add water and blend lightly. Form into a ball. Dough may be rolled out at this point, but it is easier to handle if refrigerated for 30 minutes.

On a floured board, roll out dough to a circle slightly larger than the pie pan. Gently lift and place dough into the oiled pie pan (dish). Breaks in the dough can be pinched or patched together.

For honey cheesecake: Prick dough with fork in several places, sprinkle top of pie crust with dry beans or small clean pebbles, and bake for 8 minutes in an oven preheated to 400°F (200°C, Gas mark 6). Remove beans or pebbles and bake another 2 to 3 minutes. To cook completely, leave pie crust in oven for 20 to 30 minutes, taking care not to burn.

Passover Spice Cake.

Sweet Millet Balls

Finger foods such as these dainty sweetmeats were the preferred way to serve desserts or snacks in the ancient Middle East, where there were few forks or spoons. The Children of Israel washed their hands before praying and always prayed before eating.

11/2 cups (350g) chopped dried fruit (raisins, figs, apricots, dates—1/3 cup of each is a good combination)

1 cup (225g) cooked millet (see page 21)

1/2 cup (125g) chopped walnuts

1/2 cup (125g) chopped or ground almonds

If dried fruit is unusually dry, cover and soak in boiling water for an hour. Combine chopped fruit (vary proportions to taste if desired), cooked millet, and walnuts. Shape the sticky mixture into balls about 1 inch (25mm) in diameter. Roll balls between hands until smooth. Dip the balls in chopped or ground almonds. Makes about 32 little balls. Refrigerate. This recipe is easy and fun for children.

Ashurey

Noah and his family knew that the flood was ending when a dove returned to the ark with an olive branch (Genesis 8:11). According to legend, all the remaining food was made into a sweet pudding called Ashurey.

1 cup (225g) cooked chick peas (canned may be used)

1/2 cup (125g) bulgur wheat

1/4 cup (50g) millet

1/4 cup (50g) barley, hulled or pearled

6 cups (1.8 litres) water

3/4 cup (220ml) milk

3/4 cup (175g) honey

1 tablespoon salt

1/4 cup (50g) raisins

1/4 cup (50g) figs, cut up and stemmed

1/4 cup (50g) dates, pitted and cut up

1/4 cup (50g) dried apricot pieces

1/4 cup (50g) almonds, in small pieces

1/4 cup (50g) walnut pieces

Dash of rose water (or to taste)

Yogurt or whipped cream

Cook chick peas, bulgur, millet, and barley in the water for 1 hour or until barley is tender. Add the milk, honey, salt, raisins, figs, dates, and apricots. Stir and simmer for 30 minutes. Add the almonds, walnuts, and rose water. Turn off the heat and stir. Serve hot or cold, garnished with yogurt or whipped cream. Vary proportions to taste.

Raisin, Barley, and Apricot Pudding

. . . they shall bake the grain offering.
Ezekiel 46:20

1 cup (225g) pearled barley

2 cups (60ml) water

1/2 cup (125g) dried apricots

1/2 cup (125g) white raisins (sultanas)

1/2 cup (125g) dark raisins

1/4 cup (50g) honey

1/2 teaspoon powdered ginger

1/4 teaspoon cinnamon

Yogurt

Cook the barley in 1 cup (300ml) water for 30 minutes. Drain. In a large bowl, cover the apricots and raisins (sultanas) with 1 cup (300ml) water and let sit for 10 minutes. Add the partially cooked barley, honey, and spices. Blend well. Pour the mixture into an oiled baking pan, dot with butter, and bake at 350°F (180°C, Gas mark 4) for 40 minutes. Serve warm or cold, topped with yogurt. If you wish to use hulled or hulless barley, precook barley for 45 minutes, add 11/2 cups of apple juice to mixture above and bake for 11/2 hours. Serve with yogurt if desired. This recipe provides a nutritious way to satisfy a craving for sweets and makes an excellent breakfast dish.

Honey-Fried Nuts

I went down to the garden of nuts. . . .
Song of Solomon 6:11

3/4 cup (175g) honey

1 teaspoon Fish Sauce (see page 66)

1 tablespoon vinegar or lemon juice

1 cup (225g) whole almonds or walnut halves

Butter or oil for frying

Combine honey, Fish Sauce, and vinegar or juice. Marinate the nuts in this mixture at least 2 hours, or overnight. Drain. In a small pan, heat enough oil or butter to just cover the nuts. Fry a few at a time. Cook until just golden. Remove and drain. Serve at the end of a meal, after other desserts.

Pistachio Almond Cookies

. . . a little honey, spices and myrrh, pistachio nuts and almonds.
Genesis 43:11

2 cups (450g) shelled almonds

1 cup (225g) shelled pistachio nuts

1/2 cup (150ml) grape or apple juice

1/2 teaspoon cinnamon

1 cup (225g) honey

1 teaspoon salt

Grind nuts to meal in a blender or food processor, a few at a time if necessary. Add juice to make a smooth paste. Add cinnamon, honey, and salt. Drop onto an oiled baking sheet and press into rounds. Bake in a preheated oven at 300°F (150°C, Gas mark 2) for 10 minutes or until golden. These cookies burn easily, so watch them carefully.

Opposite: Raisin, Barley, and Apricot Pudding (top) and Pistachio Almond Cookies.

Honeyed Cream

. . . honey and milk are under your tongue. . . .
Song of Solomon 4:11

1 pint (600ml) heavy (double) cream, clotted cream, sour cream (crème fraiche), or unflavored yogurt

1/4 cup (50g) honey (or more if desired)

In small bowls place individual portions of cream or yogurt. Pass around a bowl of honey so each person can stir in a few tablespoons. Serve the cream gently warmed on a cold night, whipped and cooled on a warm night. Biblical households had small wooden bowls used exclusively to serve milk and honey at the end of meals.

Almond Honey Paste

. . . behold, the rod of Aaron . . . had sprouted and put forth buds, had produced blossoms and yielded ripe almonds.
Numbers 17:8

2 cups (600ml) boiling water

1 pound (450g) almonds

5 to 8 tablespoons Amaretto or other almond liqueur

1 cup (225g) honey

1 cup (300ml) water

Few drops of rose water (optional)

2 egg whites, stiffly beaten

Pour the boiling water over the almonds and drain. Remove skins if desired. Grind nuts in a food processor or meat grinder to a smooth oily paste. (They may need to be ground a few times to achieve this consistency.) Add the Amaretto or other liqueur.

Heat the honey and water until a drop of the hot syrup in a cup of cool water will form a soft ball (240°F [116°C] on a candy (sugar) thermometer). Add the ground almonds, rose water, and almond liqueur. Remove from heat and add the egg whites. Pack into jars and refrigerate. Use as a spread on bread or cookies.

Almond Pistachio Paste

In the recipe above, subtract 1/2 (125g) cup almonds and add 1/2 cup (125g) pistachios. Add more honey to taste.

Pistachio Snow Sherbet

At the royal Persian banquets, one refreshed the palate between courses with snow sherbets.

1 quart (2.4 litres) clean, uncompacted snow

2 cups (600ml) fresh grape juice

1 cup (225g) pistachio nuts, blanched and shelled

Few drops of rose water

2 tablespoons honey (optional)

Store snow in freezer until ready to use. In a small saucepan, boil grape juice until liquid is reduced by about half. In a mortar or blender, grind pistachio nuts to a paste. Add rose water and sweeten with the honey if desired. Add nut mixture to grape syrup. When mixture has cooled, spoon over mounds of fresh, clean snow.

Fresh Berry Puree

. . . and come upon them in front of the mulberry trees.
2 Samuel 5:23

2 pounds (900g) fresh mulberries, washed (strawberries raspberries, blackberries, or boysenberries can be substituted)

1/4 cup (50g) honey (or to taste)

1/8 teaspoon salt

2 tablespoons vinegar or lemon juice

1 cup (300ml) heavy (double) cream or yogurt (optional)

Put half of the berries in a heavy saucepan with the honey, salt, and juice. Cook gently to a rich, syrupy mash, adding more honey if necessary. Fifteen minutes is about enough time for mulberries. Watch the fruit carefully for doneness. Remove from heat, cool for 15 minutes, and stir in the remaining fresh berries. Refrigerate if not serving immediately. Whip cream if desired and fold in cream or yogurt before serving.

Biblical Cheeses and Fruits

As with many foods that flourish in the same location, goat and sheep cheeses are wonderful with biblical fruits.
• Try *dates*, *apricots*, or *figs* arranged on a tray with a variety of mild, fresh *goat cheeses.*
• A cluster of grape-size *white cheese balls* can be served with clusters of red, green, and black *grapes.*
• *Watermelon* and *sheep cheese* is an unexpectedly good combination.
• *Muskmelons* go well with any *spiced* or *marinated cheese*, as does *citrus fruit.*
• Decorate a mound of *white cheese* with fresh *pomegranate seeds.*
• Dress fresh fruit Roman-style with *black pepper.* Black pepper sometimes cost the equivalent of $125 (£90) a pound in imperial Rome and was savored against the mild, sweet background of the finest fresh fruits.
• Stuff *curd cheeses* into *dates*, *figs*, and *stoned prunes.* Top each piece with an *almond* or *pistachio.*
• Spread fresh or toasted whole wheat bread with a *mild white cheese.* Top with slices of fresh *figs* or fresh or dried *dates.*
• A pita pocket stuffed with fresh *cheese* and *seedless grapes* or *Grape Honey* is a wholesome lunch or snack for a youngster.
• "Frost" a *melon slice* with *creamy yogurt cheese.*
• Pack demispoonfuls of *white cheese* into pitted *dates* or *prunes.* Deep-fry for 5 minutes. Sprinkle with *toasted almonds* and serve with hot milk flavored with *honey* and *cinnamon.*

Fresh Berry Puree
and Almond
Honey Paste
(bottom).

The Fruit Sweeteners of Antiquity: Grape Honey and Must

The grape honeys used in the ancient world were the equivalent of our unsugared jams and jellies. The natural fruit sugars are concentrated by boiling the grapes down to a pulpy syrup. Sweet grapes naturally produce a sweeter syrup with less cooking, while tart, underripe grapes produce tart grape honeys that are excellent condiments for meat and poultry.

GRAPE HONEY

4 cups (900g) stemmed grapes, preferably seedless

1/2 cup (150ml) water

Wash grapes and place in a saucepan with a small amount of water. Bring to a boil and simmer about 20 minutes or until thick. Strain if grape seeds are present. Store in sterilized jars or in refrigerator.

MUST

1 cup (225g) Grape Honey

1 teaspoon dry mustard *or* 2 teaspoons prepared mustard

Must is made by adding crushed mustard seed to grape honey. The proportions above are approximate. Experiment to find your preferred variation. See page 42 for an additional must recipe.

Figs in Red Wine and Cream

. . . with wine, grapes, and figs. . . .
Nehemiah 13:15

2 cups (600ml) sweet red wine

3 tablespoons honey

1 pound (450g) dried figs

1 cup (300ml) heavy (double) cream

Ground cinnamon

In a saucepan, bring red wine and honey to a boil. Add figs and turn down to a simmer. Simmer figs for an hour. Turn off heat and let cool. Add cream, whipped if desired, and serve in bowls with a dash of cinnamon.

Figs in Red Wine and Cream.

Apricot Curd

1/2 pound (250g) dried apricots, chopped or

6 ounces (200g) apricot leather

Water to cover

In a saucepan, cover dried apricots with water and simmer, stirring frequently, until a thick syrup is formed. Refrigerate.

Date Syrup

1/4 pound (125g) dates, pitted

1/2 cup (150ml) water

In a saucepan, combine dates and water and simmer on low heat until dates are soft. Mash dates into water and cook until a thick syrup is formed. Refrigerate.

Haroseth

This Passover fruit dish symbolizes the mortar the Hebrew slaves used in building the Egyptian pyramids.

3 cups (675g) chopped apples

3/4 cup (175g) almonds or walnuts, chopped

3/4 cup (220ml) sweet red wine or grape juice

1/2 teaspoon cinnamon

1/2 cup (125g) dates, chopped

1/2 cup (125g) raisins

Combine all ingredients. Serve immediately or chill for several hours. There are many variations of this recipe.

Suggested Menus

Egyptian Banquet Menu

The Egyptian empire was over two thousand years old when Abraham and Sarah first lived at the Pharaoh's court (Genesis 12). The Egyptians ate well, as the marshes of the Nile yielded abundant fish, waterfowl, and aquatic vegetables (such as the lotus). The well-irrigated Nile Valley exported grain throughout the ancient world, requiring supervision by provident administrators like Joseph (Genesis 41). According to biblical chronology the Hebrews lived in Egypt for four hundred years.

Three Bean Soup
Cornish Game Hens With Nuts
Duck in Grape Juice
Fried Fish in Radish Sauce
Whole Baked Garlic
Fig and Grape Salad
Cucumbers Stuffed With Barley and
*   Raisins*
Sabbath Bread or Challah
Sourdough Fig Roll
Watermelon

King Solomon's Feast

And when the queen of Sheba had seen all the wisdom of Solomon, the house that he had built, the food on his table, the seating of his servants, the service of his waiters and their apparel, his cup-bearers, and his entryway by which he went up to the houses of the Lord, there was no more spirit in her.
1 Kings 10:4, 5

All the foods in this menu are found in the Song of Solomon.

Grilled Marinated Quail
Saddle of Venison With Hot Apricot
*   Sauce*
Rack of Lamb With Must Sauce
Saffron Pilaf
Red Cabbage With Raisins
Apricot Raisin Sourdough Bread
Green Salad

Fresh Fig and Grape Salad
Saffron Cake
Hot Wine Spiced With Cinnamon

Babylonian Banquet

Belshazzar the king made a great feast for a thousand of his lords, and drank wine in the presence of the thousand.
Daniel 5:1

The fertile valleys of the Tigris and Euphrates rivers contained a number of city-states, collectively known as Mesopotamia, which was home to the world's first civilization. The descendants of Noah lived in Shinar (Genesis 11:2) and Abraham began his wanderings with Sarah from Ur, capital of the Chaldeans (Genesis 11:31). Periodically, one group within Mesopotamia such as the Babylonians rose up and conquered its neighbors. First Chronicles, 2 Chronicles, and 2 Kings record the Babylonian conquest of the Holy Land, beginning in 840 B.C.

Among the Mesopotamian writings are lists of produce from the royal garden of King Merodach-Baladan, who is twice mentioned in the Bible (Isaiah 39:1 and 2 Kings 20:12). The Mesopotamians had much the same diet as the Hebrews, with a few variations. And they were very fond of beer, a drink not mentioned in the Bible. Sesame was widely cultivated, the oil being preferred for cooking, and sesame seeds were a popular flavoring and garnish. Pistachio nuts were plentiful, and pale green pistachio wood paneled the royal palaces. The date palm was extensively cultivated, providing fruit, wine, wood, and the delectable hearts of palm among its myriad uses.

Roast Chicken Stuffed With Fried
*   Onions and Nuts*
Roast Suckling Lamb
Perch With Tahini Sauce
Sumerian Watercress
Tabbouleh Salad

Hearts of Palm With Yogurt Sesame
*   Sauce*
Date Nut Bread
Pistachio Almond Paste
Dates stuffed with white cheese, fried
*   in sesame oil*
Assorted dark and light beers

Persian Banquet

The Persians overthrew the Babylonian empire in 539 B.C. and allowed the captive Israelites to return home and reestablish Jerusalem. The Books of Ezra and Nehemiah chronicle the Persian period from 546 B.C. to 334 B.C. The Book of Esther tells of life in the elegant Persian court and the many feasts, including one lasting 180 days (Esther 1:4).

Persia was a land of luscious fruits, including the cherry, peach, plum, and apple. The walnut was called the Persian nut in honor of its presumed place of origin. Situated between the Middle and Far East, the Persians imported rice, spinach, exotic spices, and chicken from China and India to the Mediterranean area.

Persian cooking was renowned throughout the ancient world for its delicate spicing and rich sauces combining fruit and nuts. A banquet would include many wines and mountain snow sherbets topped with fruit syrups.

Caviar From the Caspian Sea
Persian Yogurt Soup With Meatballs
Poached Fish With Capers
Duck With Pomegranate Walnut
*   Sauce*
The Fatted Calf
Saffron Pilaf
Steamed Spinach
Snow Sherbet served between courses
Baked Apples With Cinnamon
Raisin Cake
Wines

Deipnosophists—Greek Banquet of the Learned

In 334 B.C., the Greeks, led by Alexander the Great, defeated the Persians and took control of their empire, including the Holy Land. The intellectual Greek culture, with its art, literature, and philosophy, profoundly influenced the Israelites. Conversely, the Greeks were very receptive to the Hebrew Scriptures and translated them. Many Greeks converted to Christianity during the time of Paul.

In dietary matters, the Greeks were concerned with health, exercise, and balance. How much one ate, in what combination of foods, and at what time of day were as important to the Greeks as the specific menu. The Greeks were fond of shrimp, rabbit, herbed broths, flax breads, black puddings, and cheesecake. Intelligent dinner conversation and good wine were as important to the educated Greeks as the food.

Sardines Grilled in Vine Leaves
Cream of Barley Soup
Savory Stew With Lentils and Raisins
Duck in Grape Juice
Baked Celery and Fennel
Mint Salad
Cheesecake
Fresh melon
A selection of wines

An Essene Vegetarian Meal

The Dead Sea Scrolls are manuscripts from the Essene religious sect. They testify to the many similarities between the early Christians and the Essenes. Jesus grew up near an Essene community, and some of the Apostles may have been Essenes. The Essenes lived in self-sufficient collectives and were primarily vegetarians. Members dressed in white for the communal meals, which usually included sprouted bread and wine.

Vegetable Soup With Whole Grains
Three Bean Soup
An assortment of Sprouted Essene
    Breads made with figs, raisins,
    seeds, and nuts
Leeks and Cabbage
Hot Goat Cheese With Fresh Herb
    Salad
Sweet Millet Balls
Wine
Pomegranates and fresh figs

Wedding Feast

On the third day there was a wedding in Cana of Galilee, and the mother of Jesus was there. Now both Jesus and His disciples were invited to the wedding.
John 2:1, 2

Assorted appetizers:
Olives
Sardines Grilled in Vine Leaves
Sabbath Fish Balls made with oil and
    water
Crown Roast of Lamb With
Pomegranate Raisin Sauce
Duckling With Must Sauce
Millet Pilaf
Three Sprout Salad
Orange, Onion, and Olive Salad
Tray of dried apricots, dates, and
    almonds
Shaped breads: braids, triangles, rolls
Apricot Raisin Sourdough Bread
Honey Wine Cake
Fresh fruit
Wine

Roman Banquet

The rise of the Roman Empire and the birth of Christianity are interwoven. Paul, the great missionary, was privileged to travel throughout the empire to the early churches because he was a Roman citizen.

The extravagance of the Roman banquet table is legendary. Influence and power were negotiated through extraordinary feasts. An impressive appetizer of peacock tongues might require the demise of two hundred birds. Laws were passed limiting the extravagance of banquets, but as might be expected, enforcement of this culinary moderation proved difficult.

Romans loved spicy foods, and their casseroles typically combined several meats, fish, poultry, cheese, vegetables, and herbs in one dish. Garum, the fermented anchovy sauce, appeared in almost every savory recipe. While the Romans introduced many dining customs and foods into their colonies, they preferred imported specialties from all corners of the known world.

Sweet Salty Eggs
Broccoli Goat Cheese Soup
Roast Ham With Sweet Sauces
Roman Beef Sauté With Onions
Grilled Fish With Garlic and Anchovy
Leeks and Cabbage
Roman Asparagus
Rose Apple Salad
Whole Wheat Sourdough Bread
Marinated Goat Cheeses
Hot wine scented with honey and
    cinnamon
Plums, apples, and roasted chestnuts
Honey-Fried Nuts

Agape Fish Dinner

The early Christians often met for fellowship meals known as Agape. In contrast to the extravagances of the pagan Romans, the Christians tried to maintain a modest and dignified tone, as they were exhorted to do in the Epistle of Jude. Fish, because it was a symbol of the early church, is thought to have been standard fare at the Agape table, along with vegetables and fresh breads.

Sardines Grilled in Vine Leaves
Barley Stew With Lentils
Honey Fried Fish
Grilled Saint Peter's Fish
Coriander Relish
Barley Wheat Sourdough Bread
Raisin Cake
Fresh grapes

Passover Dinner

Passover is one of the Jewish festivals, richest in tradition. Passover recalls the exodus of the Hebrews from Egyptian bondage under the grace of God and has become a symbol of liberation from slavery for many peoples. Jesus instructed the preparation of the Passover feast (Luke 22:8), which became known as the Last Supper. Passover incorporated an older celebration, the Feast of Unleavened Bread, retaining and elaborating the custom of eating no leavened products during the Passover week. The order of courses is based on the Roman banquet, including wine, raw vegetables, and a first course of eggs. Before and after the Passover dinner, the Passover service, or seder, is performed. The Haggadah is the book read during this time-honored religious service.

Hard-boiled eggs with saltwater dip
Raw vegetable platter: parsley, celery
*   stalks, olives, grated horseradish*
*   mixed with vinegar as a dip*
Matzoh
Pickled Fish
Rack of Lamb With Must Sauce
Green Salad of "Bitter Herbs"
Endive With Olives and Raisins
Haroseth
Passover Spice Cake
Wine or grape juice

Easter Dinner

Easter is not specifically mentioned in the Scriptures, but the celebration of the resurrection of Jesus evolved from Passover and became one of the first holy days of the early Christians. As with Passover, Easter incorporates some of the Roman dining customs. Ham, a favorite of Roman feasts, was served along with the traditional Paschal Lamb. Eggs, an ancient symbol of the rebirth of spring, became part of the Easter celebration.

Salty Sweet Eggs
Poached Fish with Capers
Saddle of Venison with Hot Apricot
*   Sauce*
Roast Suckling Lamb or Fatted Calf
Parched Wheat (Bulgur) Pilaf
Green Salad
Apricot Raisin Bread
Fresh Yogurt Cheese
Candied Beets
Honey Cake

Pentecost Dinner

Pentecost is an ancient agricultural festival that for centuries coincided with the first wheat harvest of the Holy Land, seven weeks after the first barley harvest. The entire 50 days between Passover and Pentecost were celebrated by the early Christian church with feasting, as opposed to the fasting that preceded Easter. Pentecost, considered to mark the beginning of the Christian church, was the time described in Acts 2 when the Holy Spirit came to the Apostles, as some 120 disciples gathered for the festival in Jerusalem.

Pentecost, called Shabuoth in the Jewish religion, celebrates the giving of the Ten Commandments on Mount Sinai. Dairy foods are traditionally eaten out of respect for the Commandment "Thou shalt not kill."

Yogurt With Fresh Herbs and
*   Cucumbers*
Barley Stew With Lentils
Saffron Pilaf
Hot Goat Cheese With Fresh Herb
*   Salad*
Roman Asparagus
Whole Wheat Pitas
Figs in Red Wine With Cream
Fennel Seed Cake
Toasted Almonds
Fresh Berry Puree
Wine and grape juice

Chanukah

Chanukah, the Feast of Lights, occurs around the time of the winter solstice and celebrates the miracle of lights during the liberation of Judaea from the Greek ruler Antiochus Epiphanes. The story is told in 1 and 2 Maccabees of the Apocrypha. The early Christian church held a festival of the Maccabees in August to commemorate this heroic struggle against paganism. Foods cooked in oil recall the oil used to light the eternal light in the restored Temple.

Assorted relishes: olives, pickles, and
*   radishes*
Roast Goose Stuffed With Raisins
*   and Barley*
Red Cabbage With Raisins
Goat Cheese Pancakes With Fennel
*   Seed*
Almond Paste
Onion Boards
Figs in Red Wine
Honey Cake

Sabbath Meal

The Sabbath celebrates God's creation of the world. In Exodus 31:17, God specifies that keeping the Sabbath "is a sign between Me and the children of Israel forever. . . ." Ancient wisdom rationalized that the imitation of God in His moral attributes was the measure of a righteous person. Therefore, if God rested on the

seventh day from His labors of worldly creation, should not mortals do the same? Whether Saturday or Sunday, the concept of setting aside a day for religious observance is unquestioned. The Greeks and Romans ridiculed the Hebrews and early Christians for wasting one-seventh of their lives in idleness, as this concept went against the prevailing pagan work ethic.

Traditionally, the Sabbath meals were prepared before sundown. Strict observance forbade any man, woman, child, or servant to work in the home or out. Even the farm animals rested on the Sabbath. Jesus attended synagogue and read for the Sabbath in Luke 4:16.

1. Sabbath Dinner
Sabbath Fish Balls (Use oil and water;
*   omit butter and milk)*
Chicken With Sage in a Clay Pot
Basic Barley
Figs in Red Wine
Challah
Fennel Seed Cake

2. Sabbath Lunch and Supper
Traditional Sabbath Casserole
Challah
Fresh fruit

Teaching Tools

Teachers and parents will find many projects to interest young and older children in biblical life and foods. Any of the suggestions for teachers can be done even more easily by parents at home who have fewer time limitations (especially over weekends) and more cooking equipment. Because many religious school sessions are limited to Sunday mornings, we are suggesting short-term projects whenever possible. The longer projects can be used in day schools and at home. The teacher can follow the plan of TV cooking shows by starting the project with the children in the classroom but bringing in the food at each stage (drained, risen, cooked, and so on) for the children to finish in the classroom.

In addition, congregations have incorporated biblical cooking classes into their programs of adult education and Bible study courses. Courses of varied length can be developed from the book, based on a general survey, on a particular food type such as bread, or concentrating on particular or seasonal feasts.

Dairy. Yogurt drinks, starting with a good yogurt, can be made quickly in the classroom, the work of a few minutes. Yogurt and yogurt cheese require 24-hour periods; cottage cheese, 6 hours. Yogurt cheese requires no cooking, only time to drain. Either type of cheese can be seasoned as in several of the recipes, using either freshly made or commercial varieties, offering an opportunity to create and sample a staple of the biblical diet.

Whole Grains and Beans can be sprouted in the classroom and then used for nibbling, for salads, or for bread. Bulgur wheat can be "cooked" with boiling water, eaten warm, or seasoned for a cold salad. Millet balls are another food project requiring no cooking and appealing to children. If

there is a hot plate or stove available, Honey-Fried Nuts, Pan-Roasted Wheat Berries or Chick Peas can be accomplished during a morning session. The chick peas must be soaked over the previous night to be ready for the class.

Bread making is an important learning experience and makes the many biblical references to bread more understandable as the time-honored process of leavening, kneading, and rising are not familiar to most children today. The morning class can begin with unleavened bread, matzoh, made cracker-size for easier distribution, as part of the study of the exodus from Egypt, or before Passover or Easter. Sarah's Bread and Barley Cakes illustrate unleavened breads of a primitive type that can be mixed and prepared for cooking in an hour and then finished in a frying pan over a hot plate or stove. Yeast breads, such as Date Nut Bread, have been made in the length of a 9:00 A.M. to 3:00 P.M. school day by preparing the sponge at home and bringing it to the class in a wide-mouthed thermos jar, to protect the sponge from changes in temperature. Then the dough can be mixed and kneaded by the children during the start of class. Bread dough made with sourdough sponge is quite strong and has survived kneading by many small hands, even much pulling and throwing. If a small oven is available, the risen loaves can be cooked in the classroom. If the dough is made into pitas, the cooking time will be far less, although a hotter oven will be required.

Meat, Poultry, and Fish dishes are generally more complicated, so would be suitable for older classes. But Salt Fish Vegetable Soup could be made by younger children and used with bulgur, Sarah's or Barley Bread, Sprouts, and Millet Balls or appropriate fruits for a simple biblical meal, with yogurt drinks on the side. Omit extra bulgur if making the soup.

Vegetables and Fruits offer ways for children to experience biblical food easily. Salads would be simplest, such as Onion, Olive, and Orange Salad, or Rose Apple Salad, omitting the

candied rose petals in favor of natural unsprayed petals from a local garden. Honey Onion Sandwiches would require preparing the onions a day ahead and bringing them to the classroom with the sandwich ingredients. In this, as in other recipes, different ingredients can be brought by individual children, increasing their participation.

Desserts and Sweeteners offer many possibilities. High-Fiber Fig Cake can be put together easily, while the various honey cakes can be made in schools with access to a kitchen. In the winter, Snow Sherbet would be an easy treat and could be tied in with discussions of the Persian court. Honeyed Cream is another typical, simple dessert for the shorter school session. Haroseth relates to the study of Roman ways since it originated as a Roman sauce and became part of the Passover meal. The ancient sweeteners Grape or Apricot Honey and Date Syrup can be made in a short time on a single burner. Millet Balls can be made with fruit dried by the children.

Children's Bible Meals and Snacks

Meals such as these can be used to teach children about life in biblical times.

1. *Matzoh*
Cinnamon Cheese
Chopped dates and almonds
Grape juice

2. *Yogurt Soup With Raisins*
Tabbouleh Fish Cakes
Apricot nectar diluted with water

3. *Barley and Whole Wheat*
Sourdough Bread
Lamb Shish Kebabs
Baked Onions
Dried Apricots

4. *Sabbath Fish Balls*
Lentil Pancakes with Grape Honey
Cold creamed beet and carob yogurt drinks
Watermelon

Select Bibliography

Books

Ausubel, Nathan, ed. A *Treasury of Jewish Folklore*, Crown Publishers (New York, 1948).

Berman, Louis A., *Vegetarianism and the Jewish Tradition*, KTAV Publishing House Inc. (New York: 1982).

Bothwell, Don and Patricia, *Food in Antiquity*, Praeger (New York: 1969).

Bottero, J., Cassin, E., and Vercoutter, J., *The Near East: Early Civilizations*, Delacourte Press (New York: 1965).

Bouquet, A. C., *Everyday Life in New Testament Times*, Scribner's (New York: 1954).

Bowman, Raymond, *Aramaic Ritual Texts from Persepolis*, University of Chicago: Oriental Institute Publications (Chicago: 1970).

Budge, E. A. Wallis, and King, L. W., eds. *Annals of the Kings of Assyria in the British Museum*, The British Museum, (London: 1902).

Conteau, Georges. *Everyday Life in Babylonia and Assyria*, Norton (New York: 1966).

Darby, W., Ghaliounqui, P., and Grivetti, L. *Food: The Gift of Osiris*, Academic Press (London: 1979).

Delitzen, Friedrich. *Babel and Bible*, Putnam and Sons (London: 1903).

Dimblesby, Geoffrey. *Plants and Archaeology*, Humanities Press Inc. (New York: 1967).

Dimont, Max, Jews, *God and History*, New American Library (New York: 1962).

Edwards, John. *The Roman Cookery of Apicus*, Hartley and Marks (Washington: 1984).

Forbes, R. J. *Studies in Ancient Technology*, Vols. III, IV, V, E. J. Brill (Leiden: 1955).

Ginsburg, Christian D. *The Essenes, Their History and Doctrine*, Routledge and Kegan Paul (London: 1956).

Goor, Asaph. *The History of the Rose in the Holy Land Throughout the Ages*, Massada and Am Hassefer, (Ramat-Gan: 1970, 1982).

Hedrick, U. P., ed. *Sturtevant's Edible Plants of the World*, Dover Publications (New York: 1972).

Hepper, F. Nigel, *Baker Encyclopedia of Bible Plants*, Baker Book House. (Grand Rapids: 1992).

Hoffner, Henry A. *Alimenta Hethaeorum: Food Production in Hittite Asia Minor*, American Oriental Society (New Haven: 1974).

Holm, Don and Myrtle. *The Complete Sourdough Cookbook*, Caxton Printers (Caldwell, Ohio: 1972).

Jaffrey, Madhur. *World of the East Vegetarian Cooking*, Alfred Knopf (New York: 1983).

Keating, J. F. *The Agape and the Eucharist*, AMS Press (New York: 1901).

Kenyon, Sir Frederic. *Our Bible and the Ancient Manuscripts*, Harper & Row (New York: 1958).

Kenyon, Kathleen. *Archeology in the Holy Land*, Ernest Benn Ltd. (London: 1960).

Kinard, Malvina, and Crisler, Janet. *Loaves and Fishes*, Keats Publishing (New Canaan: 1975).

King, Eleanor Anthony. *Bible Plants for American Gardens*, Dover Publications (New York: 1975).

Lehner, Ernst and Johanna. *Folklore and Odysseys of Food and Medicinal Plants*, Tudor Publishing Company (New York: 1962).

Leonard, John Norton. *The First Farmers*, Time-Life Books (New York: 1973).

Liebman, Malvina. *Jewish Cookery from Boston to Baghdad*, E. H. Seaman Publishing Co. (Miami: 1975).

Maimon, Moses Ben (Maimonides). *The Preservation of Youth*, Philosophical Library (New York: 1958).

Madza, Maidah, *In a Persian Kitchen*, Charles E. Tuttle Company (Rutland, Vermont: 1960).

Mallos, Tess. *The Complete Middle Eastern Cookbook* (New York: 1979).

Mansoor, Menahem. *The Dead Sea Scrolls*, William Eerdmans (New York: 1964).

McKibbin, Jean. *Cookbook of Foods from Bible Days* (Salt Lake City: 1971).

McNair, James. *The World of Herbs and Spices*, Robert L. Iacopi, (San Francisco: 1979).

Mellart, James, *Earliest Civilizations of the Middle East*, McGraw-Hill (New York: 1965).

Merrill, Selah, *Ancient Jerusalem*, Fleming H. Revell Company, (New York: 1908).

Miller, Madeleine S., and Lane, Jay. *Harper's Biblical Dictionary*, Harper Brothers (New York: 1952).

Murray, Margaret. *The Splendor That Was Egypt*, Philosophical Library (New York: 1949).

Nathan, Joan. *The Jewish Holiday Kitchen*, Schocken Books (New York: 1979).

Negev, Abraham. *Archaeology in the Land of the Bible*, Schocken Books (New York: 1977).

Plaut, W. G., Bamberger, B. J., and Hallo, W. W. *The Torah: A Modern Commentary*, Union of American Hebrew Congregations (New York: 1981).

Ramazani, Nesta. *Persian Cooking*, Quadrangle Press (New York: 1974).

Roden, Claudia. *A Book of Middle Eastern Food*, Vintage (New York: 1974).

Roebuck, Carl. *The World of Ancient Times*, Scribner's (New York: 1966).

Simon, Marcel. *Jewish Sects in the Time of Jesus*, Fortress Press (Philadelphia: 1967).

Short, A. Rendle. *The Bible and Modern Medicine*, The Paternoster Press (London: 1953).

Storck, John, and Teague, Walter Dorwin. *Flour for Man's Bread*, University of Minnesota Press (Minneapolis: 1952).

Strong, James. *The New Strong's Exhaustive Commentary of the Bible*, Thomas Nelson (Nashville: 1984).

Tannahill, Reay, *Food in History*, Stein and Day (New York: 1973)

Thomas, D. Winton. *Documents from Old Testament Times*, Thomas Nelson (New York: 1973).

United Bible Services. *Fauna and Flora of the Bible—Helps for Translators* (London: n.d.).

Periodicals

Arrington, L. R. "Foods of the Bible" in *Journal of the American Dietetic Association*, Volume 35, August 1959: 816–20.

Bottero, Jean. "The Cuisine of Ancient Mesopotamia" in *Biblical Archaeologist*, March 1985: 36–47.

Broshi, Magen. "The Diet of Palestine in the Roman Period—Introductory Note" in *The Israel Museum*, Vol.V, Spring 1986: 41–56.

Lumet, Henri. "The Cuisine of Ancient Sumer" in *Biblical Archaeology Review*, September 1987: 132–40.

Zimmerman, Sybil. "Housewares and Recipes from 2000 Years Ago" in *Biblical Archaeology Review*, September–October 1981: 55–58.

Index of Biblical and Historical References

Index of Food and Recipes